365 WAYS
TO MOTIVATE
AND REWARD

Your Employees Every Day—
With Little or No Money

Dianna Podmoroff, BA, MBA, CHRP

365 Ways to Motivate and Reward Your Employees Every Day—With Little or No Money

Atlantic Publishing Group, Inc. Copyright © 2005
1210 SW 23rd Place • Ocala, Florida 34474 • 800-814-1132 • 352-622-5836–Fax
Web site: www.atlantic-pub.com • E-mail sales@atlantic-pub.com

SAN Number :268-1250

International Standard Book Number: 0-910627-51-7

Library of Congress Cataloging-in-Publication Data

Podmoroff, Dianna.
  365 ways to motivate and reward your employees every day-with little or no money / Dianna Podmoroff.
      p. cm.
   Includes index.
   ISBN 0-910627-51-7 (alk. paper)
   1. Incentives in industry. 2. Employee motivation. I. Title: Three hundred and sixty-five ways to motivate and reward your employees every day-with little or no money. II. Title.

   HF5549.5.I5P58 2005
   658.3'14--dc22
                          2005015287

Print in the United States

ART DIRECTION & INTERIOR DESIGN: Meg Buchner • megadesn@mchsi.com
FRONT COVER DESIGN: Jackie Miller
BOOK PRODUCTION DESIGN: Laura Siitari of Siitari by Design • www.siitaribydesign.com

table of

CONTENTS

Chapter 3
RECOGNITION—THE KEY TO SUSTAINABLE MOTIVATION

Chapter 4
INSPIRING TIPS FOR BUILDING A HIGH-MOTIVATION WORKPLACE

Chapter 5
FREQUENTLY ASKED QUESTIONS ABOUT
REWARD AND RECOGNITION

Chapter 6
MOTIVATION 365: A MONTHLY CALENDAR

Chapter 7
MOTIVATION RESEARCH, FACTS & STUDIES

We recently lost our beloved pet "Bear," who was not only our best and dearest friend but also the "Vice President of Sunshine" here at Atlantic Publishing. He did not receive a salary but worked tirelessly 24 hours a day to please his parents. Bear was a rescue dog that turned around and showered myself, my wife Sherri, his grandparents Jean, Bob and Nancy and every person and animal he met (maybe not rabbits) with friendship and love. He made a lot of people smile every day.

We wanted you to know that a portion of the profits of this book will be donated to The Humane Society of the United States.

–Douglas & Sherri Brown

THE HUMANE SOCIETY
OF THE UNITED STATES ©

The human-animal bond is as old as human history. We cherish our animal companions for their unconditional affection and acceptance. We feel a thrill when we glimpse wild creatures in their natural habitat or in our own backyard.

Unfortunately, the human-animal bond has at times been weakened. Humans have exploited some animal species to the point of extinction.

The Humane Society of the United States makes a difference in the lives of animals here at home and worldwide. The HSUS is dedicated to creating a world where our relationship with animals is guided by compassion. We seek a truly humane society in which animals are respected for their intrinsic value, and where the human-animal bond is strong.

Want to help animals? We have plenty of suggestions. Adopt a pet from a local shelter, join The Humane Society and be a part of our work to help companion animals and wildlife. You will be funding our educational, legislative, investigative and outreach projects in the U.S. and across the globe.

Or perhaps you'd like to make a memorial donation in honor of a pet, friend or relative? You can through our Kindred Spirits program. And if you'd like to contribute in a more structured way, our Planned Giving Office has suggestions about estate planning, annuities, and even gifts of stock that avoid capital gains taxes.

Maybe you have land that you would like to preserve as a lasting habitat for wildlife. Our Wildlife Land Trust can help you. Perhaps the land you want to share is a backyard—that's enough. Our Urban Wildlife Sanctuary Program will show you how to create a habitat for your wild neighbors.

So you see, it's easy to help animals. And The HSUS is here to help.

The Humane Society of the United States
2100 L Street NW
Washington, DC 20037
202-452-1100
www.hsus.org

INTRODUCTION

If there's one topic of conversation that permeates most business productivity issues, it's employee motivation. And the usual complaint is that the employees at company XYZ are not motivated. The managers moan, "Where can I find motivated employees?" No one seems to have the answer. Does this train of thought sound familiar?

> *"Motivated employees are found in lots of other workplaces, so why can't we find and hire them to work for us? We seem to have no end of qualified applicants, so we must be doing something right in recruitment and hiring. How come we can't seem to predict which employees will turn out to be star performers?"*

Even the sharpest and most refined recruitment and hiring strategies are no match for the culprits of employee de-motivation. At the root of the problem is the fact that you don't find motivated employees; you provide motivating environments for employees.

Most employees start off with very good intentions, but if their contributions to your workplace go unnoticed and unappreciated day after day, month after month, and yes, sometimes even year after year, even the brightest star begins to fade and die away.

It's not all dismal, though; you have the power to motivate! Notice I said motivate, not coerce, force, cajole, badger or even convince. Motivation is not something that comes from the outside and it can't be faked or put-on to please someone else. Zig Ziglar said it best when he stated that his role was not to motivate anyone—people motivate themselves. His job was to enlighten people and awake an enthusiasm within themselves.

Trying to motivate someone to do something is like putting the cart before the horse. You must first create an appealing and motivating work environment, and after that, employees will do what comes natural: work hard for someone who recognizes and appreciates them. It would be pretty darn hard to come to work and do a slack job for a boss who supported you, encouraged you, respected you, and genuinely cared for you.

And that exact notion is the foundation for this book. I will talk about ways to create a motivating culture, and I will include tips and techniques and specific examples to try. These techniques, though, are simply the tip of the motivation iceberg. They are the tangible rewards, activities and recognitions that everyone sees. The real power of motivation lies in what is going on under the surface: how strong, how genuine, how real is your commitment to provide meaningful and rewarding work? Ultimately, the question that remains is:

"How motivated are you to provide a motivating workplace?"

"Money was never a big motivation for me, except as a way to keep score. The real excitement is playing the game."

DONALD TRUMP

chapter 1

A LESSON LEARNED: MY OWN DISMAL FORAY INTO MOTIVATION

"You don't have to change that much for it to make a great deal of difference. A few simple disciplines can have a major impact on how your life works out in the next 90 days, let alone in the next 12 months or the next 3 years."

JIM ROHN

When I was first out of graduate school, fresh with my MBA in hand and convinced I knew everything I needed to know about managing people, I accepted a job at a manufacturing company. My job was to create and "be" the Human Resource department. During the interview process it became clear that this company was struggling with a great many human resource issues that stemmed, in their opinion, from the fact that they had no professional human resource guidance.

Awesome, I thought. I was being handed a blank slate upon which I could work my magic. Clearly what this company needed were some HR systems and programs designed specifically for the company. I could do that.

In the first week I learned a whole lot about manufacturing, and the history of the company, and the issues management was struggling with. The first thing I learned was there were three distinct groups of people who worked there: Managers, Manager Wannabes and Employees.

The managers held the title "Manager" and talked incessantly about the problems created by the manager wannabes and employees. They, you see, were not employees—they were managers. As such, they had no responsibility for creating any problems; they just had to keep cleaning up the mess.

The manager wannabes were former employees who had been promoted to a supervisory position. This group complained incessantly about the employees and took every opportunity they could to make it clear to the employees that they wielded power and authority. What they pined for, however, was the prestige and status afforded to the managers.

Finally, the employee group: the group without

whose labor the managers and manager wannabes would have no jobs. They complained incessantly to the managers about the manager wannabes. The main complaints were that the wannabes ruled with tyrannical power and were generally incompetent in the first place.

With my firm understanding of the long-entrenched pecking order within this company, I was called to a meeting with the Director of Operations, a well-intentioned man who could not figure out why his staff was so unmotivated. Sure, they met the production rates, but employee morale was in the toilet, absenteeism was rampant, supervisors were acting like vigilantes, and the management team was overwhelmed with the difficulties. As he explained all the programs he had put in place to improve motivation, I took notes:

- Free transportation to and from work (the facility was 45 minutes out of town).

- "Family tree" in the main entrance had pictures of all the employees hanging from its branches.

- Compensation and benefits equivalent to other facilities within the company.

- Suggestion box in the lunchroom.

- Formal recognition program—employees earned points for company merchandise every month if production goals were met. (Merchandise included such things as water bottles, T-shirts and sweatshirts to market umbrellas, luggage and the coveted leather bomber jacket.)

- Annual company picnic.

- Emphasis on equality and fairness (the "keeper" of this was a manager who had been with the company since its inception. She had a photographic memory for details of who got what, what the circumstance was, what decision was made—every detail right down the color of socks the employee was wearing at the time, I'm sure. This exacting recollection was useful, but more helpful was the fact that almost every incident that had ever occurred was etched in stone as a policy to be enacted in the exact same way should that circumstance ever reoccur.)

I left the meeting ready to explore these motivation programs and perhaps improve them or develop new ones. The culture in this company was very strong, however, and, as a manager, I was quickly indoctrinated into the manager's philosophy. I analyzed the motivation programs from this perspective and concluded that the programs were excellent; the problem was the supervisors.

We took immediate steps to improve the quality of supervision. The manager wannabes who could not get on board with treating their direct reports as humans were let go, and conditions seemed to improve for a while, but in a relatively short period of time, absenteeism slowly started to creep up and morale went down again. So much for my theory about the supervisors! We tried new programs like birthday recognitions, pizza once a month, monthly newsletters, an absenteeism program where employees could earn even more company merchandise, safety recognition awards, employee of the month... You name it, we tried it.

The problem, which seems so obvious to me now, was that the attitudes and general work environment did not change. The managers were still the managers, the wannabes were still the wannabes, and the employees were still the employees. There was motivation all right; unfortunately it was aimed at keeping everyone else in check. The humanity was gone, and it wasn't until I looked at the motivation programs from an employee's perspective that I realized the magnitude of the problem:

- Free transportation. You don't pay us enough to afford and insure a car, so how else are we supposed to get to work?

- "Family tree." This is the most dysfunctional family we've ever seen, and you have pictures up there of employees who quit months, even years, ago.

- Compensation and benefits. When you explained how "great" our total compensation was you included almost $2 per hour for the "free" transportation we get!

- Suggestion box in the lunchroom. The box has no paper or pens and gets read once in a blue moon, and if a suggestion is implemented, one of the wannabes will likely get the credit.

- Formal recognition program. The production goals aren't goals, they are what we need to produce; period. The manager gets the sales forecast, determines what we need to produce, and we do it. And our work gets other people rewarded. We make the production goal and everyone else in the company gets points. Why bother? Just give us the stuff so we'll wear your name all over town and then everyone's happy.

- Annual company picnic. This one's quite fun, but we get it every year regardless of how well we do; the managers certainly wouldn't miss the opportunity.

- Emphasis on equality and fairness. I just love it when I ask for a special consideration and it's denied only because someone three years ago asked for the same thing and it didn't work out. Or I come to work on time every day and I get treated exactly the same as the guy who misses a quarter of his shifts

I know, I know, I'm mortified when I look back on this and think how completely snowed I was. I saw only what was on the surface (the tip of the motivation iceberg) and had no appreciation for the enormity of what was lurking below. The attitudes, beliefs and values of company management formed the foundation of this enormous issue, and since only the reactions (the attempts to motivate) were visible, those were identified as the problem.

Remember, too, I came into the company as a complete newbie. I had no preconceived notions or ideas about the way things had always been, but I was so quickly absorbed into the strong counter-motivating culture that I didn't even realize it was happening. This brings the challenge of motivation into perspective. Imagine how difficult it is for people who work in, and perhaps built, the company environment to identify the underlying issues that de-motivate, let alone come up with solutions that address what is both above and below the surface. Motivation is not an issue that can be fixed with a "solution." Workplace motivation is bred and nurtured and it involves all parties and all aspects of the work environment.

Motivation encompasses the entire scope of workplace activities, from the actual work being performed to who is performing the work and how the work is managed—all of these aspects significantly contribute to the health of the workplace and thus to the level of what is commonly termed employee motivation. This is a complex topic that affects the performance of the company as a whole and impacts the level of satisfaction of each and every employee. My hope is that after reading this book you will have a newfound appreciation for the importance and complexity of workplace motivation and that you will be armed with the tools you need to start building a high-motivation workplace within your organization.

The benefits of a highly motivated workforce are very evident and the rewards your company will reap are very worth pursuing. The transformation will not happen overnight, but when it does, you can expect the following results:

- Renewed motivation, morale and meaning at work.

- Improved personal/professional performance.

- Enhanced teamwork, trust and fun at work.

- Increased energy and resilience to stress.

- Enriched quality of work/life balance.

- Heightened workplace creativity and humor.

- Enlightened and inspired organizations.

- Enhanced retention through recognition.

- Elevated enthusiasm and involvement with interactive sessions.

- Deepened appreciation for internal and external customers.

- Improved customer care and service delivery.

- Decreased absenteeism, burnout and turnover.

- Improved productivity and organization.

The benefits of well-directed motivation are obvious and compelling and, thus, my intention with this book is twofold:

1. To heighten your awareness of and appreciation for the issues lurking beneath the surface of your workplace and give you tools to build a strong motivation foundation.

2. To inspire you with some specific tools, techniques and strategies for building a high-motivation workplace full of motivated employees.

chapter 2

MOTIVATION—WHAT IT IS, WHAT IT ISN'T

"Motivation is universal; motivators are individual."

Human beings are pre-wired to be motivated. Something gets us up every morning. Even if the only reason we get up is because we're hungry, we're still motivated to satisfy our need to eat. In the workplace, motivation is more complex, and what motivates some does not motivate others. Therein lies the problem that managers struggle with on a daily basis. Often deemed "attitude" problems, these issues are usually problems related to untapped or misdirected motivation. In order to correct the problem, it is important that managers and leaders understand exactly what motivation is. Once you understand the forces at work, you will have a much easier time applying the techniques and tips presented in the subsequent chapters.

There are many different theories of motivation that have become intertwined with current management practices. In order to get a solid grasp on this concept of motivation, it is important that we revisit, and in some cases learn about, some of these foundational theories to understand why we have come to view workplace motivation as we have and from where some of the common solutions to motivational problems stem.

MOTIVATION THEORIES

Abraham Maslow

The desire to satisfy a need is what Dr. Abraham Maslow identified as the impetus for our attitudes and actions. According to Maslow, we have five levels of need. The first, and most basic, level is the need for Survival. The next level up is Safety, and together these two levels represent our basic needs. Luckily most of us reading this book do not have to spend too much time focusing on satisfying food, clothing, shelter and safety needs, and this puts us in the enviable position of pursuing higher-level needs that contribute to overall quality of life.

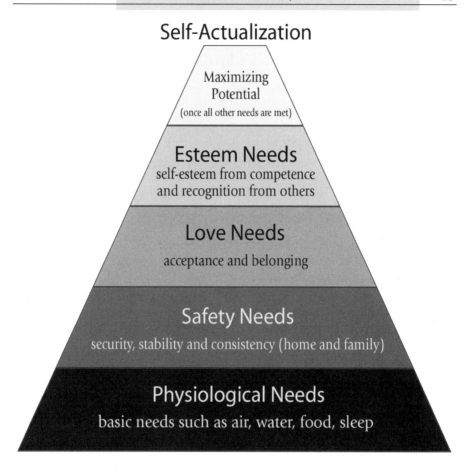

Since we spend nearly one-third of our adult lives at work, it stands to reason that we want our workplace to be a source of need fulfillment. When that happens, our lives are full and enriched and we can focus our attention on finding meaning through work; when it doesn't happen, we are so preoccupied with finding other ways to satisfy our needs that we are never truly "present" at work. Our productivity, engagement, morale, enthusiasm, interest and enjoyment all suffer. Put a whole bunch of unfulfilled people in one workplace and look out!

Many recognition programs are based on Maslow's theory. Attempts to satisfy needs related to social interaction and self-esteem are commonly put in place. One of the most common motivation tools used today is the "employee of the month" or some variation thereof. These types of tools are a direct response to our belief that employees seek workplace recognition of their accomplishments and this recognition helps satisfy self-esteem needs. The theory follows that if we are not recognized for our achievements, then we are not growing and fully developing as individuals and our attentions may wander away from the tasks at hand.

Maslow's work is often considered the foundation from which other motivation theories grew, and many of these theorists support a downward cycle of employee motivation when particular needs are not met.

Frederick Herzberg—Hygiene and Motivational Factors

As mentioned, Maslow is considered the "father" of motivational theory, and most of the subsequent work on motivation has been done with his model in mind.

Frederick Herzberg's Hygiene and Motivational Factors theory was the next to emerge. He took Maslow's ideas and concentrated on human needs at work, not for life in general. His theory centered on the notion that humans have two types of needs:

1. Needs related to hygiene (simple base-line, factors).

2. Needs related to motivational factors.

Hygiene factors are those elements of a job that are related to working conditions, and motivational factors relate to elements that enrich one's job.

Herzberg's Hygiene and Motivational Factors

Hygiene Factors	Motivational Factors
Policies and practices	Recognition
Compensation	Achievement
Job security	Advancement
Coworkers	Growth
Supervision	Responsibility

Hygiene factors themselves are not motivating, but if they are not adequate, they are sources of dissatisfaction. All hygiene factors must be met in order for motivational factors to be satisfying. Herzberg coined the term "job satisfaction" and referred to it as the designing of jobs with built-in motivational factors.

The combination of hygiene and motivation factors can result in four conditions.

High Hygiene	Employees work to make a living. They have few complaints but are not highly motivated.	The ideal situation where employees are highly motivated and have few complaints.
Low Hygiene	This is the worst situation where you have unmotivated employees who have lots of complaints.	Employees are motivated but have a lot of complaints. The job itself provides excitement and challenge but the job conditions do not meet minimal expectations.
	Low Motivation	**Motivation**

The response to Herzberg's Two Factor Theory within corporations was to concentrate on the actual design of jobs being performed. A great deal of attention was given to making sure people had jobs that were inherently satisfying. The burden of workplace motivation was solidly entrenched as the responsibility of management and they were tasked with making sure employee needs were taken of.

These theories made sense and were empirically supported but, unfortunately, workplace motivation did not necessarily improve as a result of any changes these theories supported. Some people were motivated, some weren't, and it seemed the increased understanding of motivation was doing little to help the practical application of motivation at work.

So, a whole new generation of motivational theorists emerged. These theorists found that Maslow's hierarchy did not work in the real world. The needs that Maslow identified seemed well grounded, but most people skipped around through the levels depending on their circumstances, stage of life, interests, etc. They cited many examples that were not congruent with the hierarchy. If you consider a starving artist who sacrifices certain survival and safety needs in order to pursue his passion, or a physician who gives up her practice to work with children in Africa whose parents have AIDS, then you can understand that a hierarchical setup is not consistent with human behavior.

The difficulty with Herzberg's Two Factor Theory was with the overlap of hygiene and motivation factors. They were not quite as black and white as the theory suggested, and dissatisfaction with one factor could have very different effects with different people. Some people did not respond to increased recognition (motivation factor) but instead focused on advancement. Others were willing to sacrifice compensation (hygiene factor) for work that provided a great deal of personal satisfaction. Again, the theories fell short of applying to the workforce in general.

Clayton Alderfer— Existence/Relatedness/Growth (ERG) Theory of Needs

To address the shortcomings in Maslow's model, Clayton Alderfer developed the Existence/Relatedness/ Growth (ERG) Theory of Needs. He took Maslow's ideas and created three groups of needs that individuals could move through simultaneously. He also proposed that different people would move through the needs in different orders.

Existence/Relatedness/Growth (ERG)

Need	Example
Existence	This group of needs is concerned with providing the basic requirements for material existence. It includes Maslow's Survival and Safety needs. Working to earn money to buy food, clothing and shelter satisfies existence needs.
Relationship	This group of needs centers on the desire to establish and maintain interpersonal relationships. These needs are related to Maslow's Social needs. Since we spend a significant time at work, we look to coworkers and colleagues to satisfy many of our social needs.

Growth	These needs are satisfied through personal growth and development opportunities. They are related to the group of needs Maslow referred to as Esteem and Self-Actualization. Many of us look to marry our personal meaning and purpose with our professional lives, and, thus, our job becomes a main source of satisfaction or dissatisfaction.

According to Alderfer, people can move simultaneously through the needs, but lower-level (existence) needs will take on greater importance when higher-level need achievement is frustrated. This dynamic is called "frustration-regression" and works like this: If a higher-level need is left unfulfilled or appears unattainable, the individual will seek out lower-level needs because they are easier to satisfy. This regression exacerbates the frustration because less time is spent trying to pursue those needs that result in the most personal satisfaction.

Practical solutions based on this theory concentrated on making sure the lower-level needs were satisfied for everyone before moving on to higher needs. The intention was to create workplaces that did not frustrate or hinder employees' search for satisfaction.

Vroom's Expectancy Theory of Motivation

Vroom's theory is based on the idea that individuals have expectations about outcomes and that, in terms of work, there are two main groups of outcomes:

Intrinsic outcomes/motivators

This is how interesting, challenging and meaningful the job is.

Extrinsic outcomes/rewards

Work-related conditions, salary and security are the expected outcomes or rewards.

Vroom's theory assumes that behavior results from conscious choices and that people are naturally wired to maximize pleasure (positive outcomes) and minimize pain (negative outcomes). The expectancy theory says that individuals have different goals/desires/dreams and they can be motivated if they believe all of the following to be true:

1. There is a correlation between their effort and performance—the harder they work, the greater their performance.

2. Greater performance will result in a desired outcome (reward).

3. That outcome (reward) will satisfy a need (desire/dream/goal).

4. The desire to satisfy that need is strong enough to justify the increased effort.

For the Expectancy Theory to work, all four of those beliefs must be present for an employee to motivate him or herself to put forth the necessary effort.

The easiest way to understand the Expectancy Theory is with an example as follows:

> Bobby goes to work every day and earns a decent living. Raises at his company are given out on a yearly basis, based solely on tenure (length of time with the company). Bobby does not have to put forth any excess effort to earn his raise, he simply has to show up for work every day for another year. For this company, pay increases are not motivating and they have no ability to motivate.

Susan also goes to work every day and earns a decent living. At Susan's company, wage increases are based on performance. Each employee sets objectives for the year and they are evaluated on how well they achieved their goals. Because the employees are involved in the goal-setting process, they are excited about and committed to completing them. They also know that pay raises are linked directly to performance.

At Susan's company, the employees are doubly motivated:

1) They are intrinsically motivated to achieve goals they have set for themselves.

2) There is potential for a monetary reward if they achieve their goal. Money is a motivator in this company but it is important to note it is not the sole motivator.

As you can see, the performance-based models of compensation are a direct result of Vroom's theory, as are all the other incentive programs that are so popular today.

Graves and Beck—Spiral Dynamics

A "new" theory that has direct implications for workplace motivation is Spiral Dynamics. Spiral

Dynamics explores the core values and thoughts that drive an individual's beliefs and actions. The original concept began in the 1930s with the work of Dr. Clare Graves, but he died before publishing his theory and it remained in the realm of personality psychologists until Dr. Don Beck wrote a book entitled *Spiral Dynamics Integral* based on his extended version of the Graves' original biopsychosocial theory.

> *"I am not saying in this conception of adult behavior that one style of being, one form of human existence is inevitably and in all circumstances superior to or better than another form of human existence, another style of being. What I am saying is that when one form of being is more congruent with the realities of existence, then it is the better form of living for those realities. And what I am saying is that when one form of existence ceases to be functional for the realities of existence, then some other form, either higher or lower in the hierarchy, is the better form of living."*
>
> DR. CLARE W. GRAVES

In Beck's model, Graves' value systems are combined with memes (cognitive or behavioral pattern that can be transmitted from one individual to another) to form eight different vmemes (value memes), and by discovering which vmeme an individual operates under, others can relate better to that individual.

The memes are presented in a helix model that indicates the movement through the levels but also recognizes that people may move back down or stay fixed depending on life circumstances. In Spiral Dynamics, the goal is for all people to continue their movement upward in the spiral, continually expanding their thoughts and consciousness, but that existential side of Spiral Dynamics will not be explored in this book.

Eight Value Systems/vMemes that have emerged to date:

vMemes	Description
BEIGE	Instinctive/Survivalist Do what you must to survive.
PURPLE	Magical/Animistic Use rituals and have a mystical sense of cause and effect.
RED	Impulsive/Egocentric Emphasize cunning and doing what you want to do. Strong prevail and the weak serve.

vMemes	Description
BLUE	Purposeful/Authoritarian Desire-ordered existence and enforce principles based on what is "right." Controlled by a higher power.
ORANGE	Strategic/Achievement Oriented Take advantage of all opportunities and strive for success. Make things better and bring prosperity.
GREEN	Egalitarian/Community Oriented Demand human rights and develop caring communities. Look for affiliation and sharing.
YELLOW	Integrative View the world as integrated systems and emphasize flexibility. Change is the norm.
TURQUOISE	Holistic Combine mind and spirit to experience life's complete existence. The world is a delicate balance that is in jeopardy in human hands.

Essentially, Spiral Dynamics was developed in order to help us understand:

- How people think about things (as opposed to "what" they think).

- Why people make decisions in different ways.

- Why people respond to different motivators.

- Why and how values arise and spread.

- The nature of change.

Spiral Dynamics is the theory that attempts to address why some motivation programs work for some people and in some situations. The other main theories attempt to uncover the one universal method for motivating people whereas Spiral Dynamics takes a much more individual approach to motivation. Because it has been my experience that people do respond to motivational methods very differently, the premises of this theory are evident in many of the constructs of workplace motivation presented in this book.

All of these theories of motivation are useful for constructing an overall answer to a fundamental workplace issue: How to put the right people in the right positions and help them reach maximum satisfaction and achieve maximum productivity.

That really is what motivation is all about. You can try and try and try some more to motivate someone to do something, but if he or she has no desire (gets no satisfaction) to do the task, then you are beating a dead horse.

Effective motivation requires shifting your mindset and understanding that you can't make anyone do anything. What you can do is create the right set of circumstances for a motivating workplace to emerge. That is what this book will teach you to do.

You can't coerce motivation, but you can, and should, foster it.

WORKPLACE MOTIVATION

Many people have tried to define motivation, but we are focusing on motivation in the workplace. For our purposes, motivation is the inner force that drives individuals to achieve personal and professional goals.

Why is workplace motivation so important? Because we need motivated employees in order to survive. Motivated employees are more productive and they infuse positive energy into the work environment. There is nothing more de-motivating than an unhappy workplace, and negativity is an insidious and nefarious opponent in the struggle for a high-motivation work environment. Add to that the fact that what motivates employees changes constantly, and it is no wonder workplace motivation is one of the most complex issues managers deal with.

Because workplace motivation is on the minds of organizational leaders everywhere, there is considerable misinformation about motivation that needs to be cleared up. The following are some of the most common yet terribly inaccurate notions that managers have regarding employee motivation.

Common Motivation Myths

"Money is the universal motivator."

While this is a common belief, it is not true. Unfair or inadequate compensation is a significant factor in employee dissatisfaction, but good or extra compensation does not encourage people to be more motivated than  they already are. Employee motivations are highly sophisticated and complex, and your job is to figure out what motivates whom and then deliver it.

> *"I am an upbeat, motivational kind of person, and I can motivate others."*

As much as we would like it to be true, no one can really motivate anyone else; they have to motivate themselves. What you can do is create a motivating environment for each of your employees.

> *"The best motivator I know is fear; fear of losing their job should motivate anyone."*

Fear may motivate in the very short-term, but it does nothing to enhance workplace harmony, and it goes a long way toward creating employee dissatisfaction. No one wants to work for a boss who is threatening and intimidating (at least not for long), and you'll find yourself with a steady stream of new and untrained employees if this is your tactic of choice.

> *"I know what motivates me, so I know what motivates my employees"*

Wrong! Everyone is motivated by different things at different times. What works for you may or may not work for your employees, and what works for them today may or may not motivate them tomorrow. Motivation isn't simple but it is so worth the trouble of finding out what individual employee's triggers are.

"Increased job satisfaction means increased job performance."

While I've alluded to this relationship throughout the book so far, the relationship between job satisfaction and job performance is not 100 percent correlated. Just because an employee is motivated to do a good job and perform to his or her potential, does not mean that he or she will perform to the expectations of the organization. There are many other factors that a company's management must attend to, such as aligning workplace goals with personal goals, ensuring employees have access to the tools and resources required to do a great job, and communicating expectations clearly, concisely and consistently. Providing a motivation-rich environment serves as the foundation for a high-performance workplace.

I'm sure you have espoused one or more of these ideas, and they are very much a part of mainstream managerial thought. The problem is they are also some of the main reasons why workplace motivation continues to frustrate and incense managers from every industry and every type of organization. By virtue of being aware of these common pitfalls, you can start to combat them within your organization right now. However, knowing what motivation is not is only the first step. Now you need to develop a solid understanding of what motivation is and why companies and researchers across the world are so interested in the subject.

EMPLOYEE MOTIVATION—TWO PERSPECTIVES

We have already defined motivation as the inner force that drives individuals to achieve personal and professional goals, but employee motivation must also be viewed from two different perspectives: internal and external motivators.

Internal Motivators

The internal motivators are what influence and propel an individual to pursue a certain job, type of career, education or other activity. These inner drives provide people with their most basic form of satisfaction. A person who feels an overwhelming desire to be a musician will never be completely fulfilled in an

office job regardless of the motivation tips and tricks used. Or the person who desires order and structure will never find complete fulfillment in a job that is unstructured. In order to provide a high-motivation workplace, you must be aware of, and sensitive to, these base line motivators that affect your employees on a day-to-day basis.

Internal motivators: Aspects of work that generally compel a person to decide to seek a particular type of employment in a particular industry.

These internal motivators are resistant to change or outside influence. This is why it is so crucial to build an environment and culture that understands and respects the different motivational forces of its employees at different times. When an employee is working at a job he or she is highly interested in or passionate about, your job as manager/motivator/coach is that much smoother. Rather than embarking on an uphill battle trying to mold an employee into one who loves his or her position, who is inwardly compelled to achieve excellence for you, and whose own goals are well aligned with the company's goals, you need to create a workplace that is dedicated to finding out what its employees need and then commit to providing it.

The simplest way to approach the task is to hire for motivational fit in the first place. If you hire people who possess internal motivational factors that are easily satisfied through the type of work offered, the goals of your organization, or the type of management you provide, then achieving a high-motivation workplace is not too difficult.

Hiring the right person for the right job is always the goal, but we know that the selection is far from perfect, so when we have employees who are struggling to find their motivation, we need to create flexibility in our workplace and accommodate those individuals the best we can. We can't change anyone's current internal motivators but we can provide options that help the person to find an internally motivating role within the company.

> *"An empowered organization is one in which individuals have the knowledge, skill, desire and opportunity to personally succeed in a way that leads to collective organizational success."*
>
> STEPHEN R. COVEY

The role of Internal Motivators is the focus of the first section of this book: *Building a Strong Motivation Foundation.*

External Motivators

The external motivators consist of those things that the world offers in response to an individual's inner drives. These can be considered the enticements an employer offers to its employees such as salary, benefits, recognition and advancement. These external motivators are what we commonly think of when we talk about factors of job satisfaction that improve employee motivation.

> **External motivators: Aspects of work that generally compel a person to seek or maintain employment with a particular company.**

Basic External Motivators

- Opportunity to work and apply special gifts and abilities in an employment setting.

- Wages that enable employees to provide themselves basic necessities and some luxuries, such as the purchase of a home or travel.

- Means to save for and enjoy retirement.

- Provision of medical and other insurance coverage.

- Camaraderie with coworkers.

- Recognition of work done well.

- Acknowledgment and possible reward for special contributions.

- Opportunity for advancement.

- Opportunity for self-development.

- Opportunity for continuous learning (improve skills/knowledge, education).

- Realization of one's full potential.

Remember, however, these external motivators are not direct substitutes for an employee's inner drives, but, when employees are working in positions that are not the best fit for them in terms of their internal motivators, these external aspects of a job can and need to be used as mitigating factors.

A discussion of effective and proven external motivators forms the basis for the second section of this book: Inspiring Tools for Building a High-Motivation Workplace.

WHAT EMPLOYEES FIND MOTIVATING

GoalManager (**www.goalmanager.com**) performed an Employee Motivation Survey in 2000 and asked, "What do you like about your current job? What are the things that keep you there?"

These are the responses:

EMPLOYEE MOTIVATION

Motivators	Percent
People and work environment.	66%
The management cares about me./Good relationship with management.	33%

Motivators	Percent
Challenging and exciting job.	33%
Flexibility.	24%
Salary.	19%
Autonomy and creative freedom with job.	16%
Training and learning opportunities.	13%
Stock options.	9%
I like the product/technology.	9%
Teamwork.	8%
I can express my ideas and management listens.	8%
Perks: Company outings, lunches, early outs, travel, dress code, etc.	8%
We have great benefits.	6%
Absence of hierarchy and red tape.	5%
I can use my skills.	5%
Recognition.	4%
I like my commute.	4%
I like working with our clients.	3%

NOTE: The percentages will not total 100 percent because respondents were not limited to one choice.

It is important to note that "People and work environment" is cited as the number-one source of satisfaction for employees at work. What this means is that attention needs to be placed on building an environment and culture that supports people and recognizes their individualism. Work is all about the people. You can develop the fanciest and most sophisticated programs for enticing people to work in the company's best interest, but if you don't place value on the best interests of your people, then all is for naught. Simply put: Your company is your people; value them and the rest will fall into place.

> *"Continuous, supportive communications from managers, supervisors and associates is too often underemphasized. It's a major, major motivator."*
>
> JIM MOULTRUP, MANAGEMENT CONSULTANT

BUILDING A STRONG MOTIVATION FOUNDATION

> *"Everything about business comes down to PEOPLE. Where in business can we escape the impact of human care, human creativity, human commitment, human frustration and human despair? There is no reason for anything in business to exist if it does not serve the needs of people."*
>
> BRUCE CRYER, RE-ENGINEERING THE HUMAN SYSTEM
> (A CONFERENCE PRESENTATION)

When we talk about motivation, we need to remember that we are talking about motivating individual people who each bring a unique set of skills and other personal factors with them to work every day. To build a strong foundation for a motivating culture, you need to understand the power and complexity of the internal factors that motivate each of these peoples' behavior.

Using our iceberg analogy, the internal motivators are the core factors that lay beneath the surface of any workplace environment. These core factors can either support motivation and boost moral, job-satisfaction, productivity and profitability or they can literally sink the entire organization. An iceberg that doesn't have a strong foundation will eventually melt away, but those that have deep roots can remain floating for centuries. For organizations, what determines the difference is the level of commitment to providing a motivating work environment that supports rather than quells its employee's natural motivation to do a good job. Yes, that's right. Employees are naturally motivated to do a good job. People don't take on tasks or responsibilities with the intention of doing them poorly. When they do a poor job, it is not because of a lack of motivation, but it can be misdirected or misguided motivation.

If people are naturally motivated to do a good job, why

do managers from all industries, all sizes of business, and all organizational structures continue to ask: How do you motivate people? How can we motivate our people toward improved productivity? How can we motivate for more effective performance?

They ask these questions because they have yet to accept that people are already motivated. They just might not be motivated to move in the "right" direction or they might not have the "right" motivators; but motivated they are.

People are always motivated and they will remain so as long as they are alive.

By asking the question, "How do you motivate employees?" you are approaching the problem from the wrong perspective. The question begs to be answered with a one-size-fits-all solution; everyone is looking for that one perfect methodology that is guaranteed to work. Managers want to know the secret formula, for the belief is that if they do something, then magically employees will do what they want, in the way they want it, and enjoy doing it to boot. Unfortunately, given all the research and brain-power of the talented individuals who have worked toward this end, if a motivational panacea existed, it would have been found by now. Job enrichment, incentive programs, management by objective, self-directed work teams, performance-based pay, participative management; I could go on and on. These systems have all been proposed, and hailed, as the ultimate method to achieve motivation-rich environments with soaring productivity. Have any of them proven that they are the answer? No. And we can keep looking for that one miracle cure for what we term "lack of motivation" but we will never find it.

Why won't we find the cure? Because each of these systems, and any others that we come up with in the future, work extremely well for some, modestly for others, and not at all or negatively for the rest. People who are intensely competitive may respond well to performance-based pay, but for those who are more interested in working as a team and collaborating on projects, performance-based pay is a dismal failure. The application of performance-based pay is not the problem; the problem is that it is not motivating to all people at one time nor is it motivating to some people all of the time. What inevitably happens, though, is the organization's leaders decide that performance-based pay does not work and they go on a never-ending search for a method that will work. They jump from one system to the next, not realizing that the changing systems are causing as much, if not more, problems for their employees and managers.

When we talk about motivation, it's not just employees we have to consider—the managers and leaders are also influenced by the changes. Their motivational levels change from time to time and from circumstance to circumstance, so when you hop from one motivational system to the next, you affect your own and all managers' performance as well. Managers, just like their subordinates who were content with the old system, may respond negatively or not at all to the changes and they will vary in their ability to apply the new system effectively. Add to that the fact that employees who were considered motivated and productive under the old system may become "unmotivated" and unhappy with the changes, and you have the exact reason why trying to find a motivational cure-all will never work. The act of looking for an answer to the question, "How do you motivate employees?" puts you in a vicious cycle where some of the people are happy some of the time but no one is happy all of the time.

When tackling the issue of employee motivation, you need to reframe your question:

How Should Manager X
Manage Employee Y to Do What?

Four Interrelated Work Systems

When you restructure your approach to employee motivation and ask, "How should Manager X manage

Employee Y to do what?" you acknowledge the four main contributors to workplace motivation and performance:

1. **Management Methods**

   The managerial policies and practices accepted and endorsed by the organization, its values and culture.

2. **The Management**

   The beliefs, values, personality, capabilities, etc., that influence the actions of each manager, leader and supervisor within the organization.

3. **The Managed**

   The beliefs, values, personality, capabilities, etc., that influence the way each employee within the organization desires to be managed and his or her reactions to the current management style.

4. **The Work**

   The actual work that needs to be done within the organization to ensure sustainability and/or profitability.

"Choose a job you love and you will never have to work a day in your life.

CONFUCIUS

For a motivation-rich culture to emerge, all four of these factors must be aligned for each and every employee within the company. That is no small task, and that is why motivation continues to be one of the hottest managerial topics to date.

If you think of these systems as cogs in the wheel of the entire management system, you begin to see that if any one of them falls out of sync, the system as a whole suffers.

In order to fully appreciate the impact of each of the systems, let's examine each one and the implications for workplace motivation separately.

"There must be congruency between the character of the work to be done, the psychology of the person who is managing, the psychology of the people being managed, and the methods and procedures of management."

FROM THE HISTORICAL COLLECTION OF THE WORK OF
DR. CLARE W. GRAVES, WILLIAM R. LEE, AUGUST 2003

MANAGEMENT METHODS

Management Methods are those practices within the organization's toolkit that managers use to oversee, supervise, direct, reward and correct subordinates' work and behavior. There are many management methods available that have been designed and developed to address workplace motivation. Most workplaces adopt a mix of two or three of these methods that best suits the organization's values, beliefs and goals. The mistake, as we have discussed already, is to assume that by adopting or adapting one or some of these methods, you will achieve workplace motivation nirvana.

You must not forget that the method of management is but one of the four interrelated dynamics operating within any workplace at any time. Therefore, if you attack motivational issues by addressing only one aspect of the workplace dynamic, you will not see the broad scope results you are hoping for. What you do need to have is a good understanding of how these various management methods work and to what aspects of employee motivation they most appeal. When you understand why these programs have been proposed, you can then decide which ones to apply in which situations and with which employees.

Here is a summary of some of the most popular management methods intended to increase employee motivation and performance:

Management by Objective

Management by Objective (MBO) is a management method developed by Peter Drucker which advocates a participative goal-setting process that actively involves managers and subordinates at every level of the organization. All employees work on objectives that are directly tied to organizational goals and these individual objectives form the basis of the performance review process.

The key elements of MBO are:

1. Effective planning and goal setting by top management.

2. Setting of individual goals that are directly related to the organization's goals.

3. Employees are given autonomy in developing and selecting means for achieving objectives.

4. Employee performance in relation to objectives is regularly reviewed.

The principal behind MBO is that it encourages employees to appraise their own performance through a process of shared goal setting and evaluation. Employees understand the goals of the organization and they see how their performance affects the company as a whole, thus creating a group of individuals who all have one higher purpose in mind. MBO creates a link between top management's strategic thinking and the strategy's implementation lower down. Responsibility for objectives is passed from the organization to its individual members.

SMART Goals

Closely related to MBO is the development of SMART goals:

Specific: the target is clearly defined.

Measurable: the target state has a quantitative component that can be verified numerically.

Appropriate: the employee has the means and resources available to accomplish the goal or meet the objective.

Realistic: the employee, after considering likely extenuating circumstances, has a reasonable chance of success.

Time-bound: the target state has a specified time for completion.

The principle behind Management by Objective is to increase the motivational factors such as autonomy, responsibility, and direct involvement in setting work goals. Traditional workplaces are typically driven by upper management and directives, strategies, objectives, etc., are handed out from the top down: the higher the position within the corporate hierarchy, the more responsibility and autonomy. MBO seeks to drive the decision making downward, allowing employees at all levels of the organization to contribute meaningfully to goal setting.

Job Enrichment/Job Rotation

Job Enrichment

Job enrichment is a type of job redesign that is intended to address the effects of boredom, lack of flexibility, and employee dissatisfaction that result from work tasks that are repetitive and highly directed. We know that responsibility and autonomy are important job satisfaction factors, so with job enrichment, the scope of a job is vertically expanded to provide a greater variety of tasks and add tasks that require self-sufficiency.

This management method stems from Herzberg's work in the 1950s, and vertical job enrichment adds more authority, accountability, degree of difficulty and specialization to an individual's work. By doing so, motivational factors such as responsibility, achievement, growth and learning, advancement and recognition are further developed. The principle behind the method is that by enriching a job the individual increases his or her job satisfaction and thus experiences motivation that the organization considers positive.

Job Rotation

Job rotation is the movement between different jobs in order to increase interest and motivation. One day a person may be working in one part of the factory and the next day they may work in a different part. The advantage of this rotation is it helps employees avoid boredom as they are doing  different jobs all the time and learning new skills. Job rotation is similar to job enlargement in that it widens the activities of a worker by switching around a range of work.

Participative Management

Participative Management is the idea of utilizing the knowledge, strengths, creativity and ingenuity of all employees within an organization and not simply relying on the managers and supervisors to direct work. With participative management, companies are asking workers, in groups and teams, to get involved in making suggestions, setting goals, improving methods, solving problems, and enhancing the quality of the company's products and services. The goal of participative management is to create high-performance teams capable of managing their operating routines and it is based on the belief that both companies and people benefit when managers and employees actively participate in decisions that affect them and their organizations.

The common benefits that proponents of participative management cite include:

- It encourages better communication and greater employee involvement in day-to-day activities and the long-range performance of a business.

- It improves effectiveness and increases productivity by giving managers and employees the necessary tools needed to participate more fully in the workplace.

- It enables staff, at all levels, to find practical solutions and design better business practices for their own companies.

- It helps create a positive work environment where everyone can contribute new ideas and provide constructive input.

- It offers managers and employees a renewed sense of pride and ownership in their organizations and accomplishment in their professional lives.

Participative Management is a synthesis of several management theories, and the basic principle of this management model is that it requires participation from all of the employees and managers to actively pursue a common goal.

Performance-Based Pay

This management method seeks to enhance employee motivation and productivity by sharing the financial results of enterprise performance with employees. In essence, performance pay is based on paying the worker for his or her unique value, rather than assessing a value to the job itself. Such schemes fall into four broad categories:

- Individual-based or based on individual performance, such as incentive schemes and sales commissions.

- Profit sharing, which applies to all or most of the employees.

- Gain sharing measured by a pre-determined performance formula, applicable to all or groups of employees. The performance measure may be profit or some other objective such as productivity.

- Employee-share ownership schemes.

The following is a description of the most common forms of performance-based pay:

Gain Sharing

This compensation method divides the results of improved performance between the employer and employees. If a department increases productivity over

a certain period, then a percentage
of that increased productivity
is attributed to company gains
and is shared among employees.
The assumption is that the better
use of human resources results
in improved performance and
the productivity gains are then
shared with those responsible: the
employees. The gains are typically
distributed according to an agreed,
pre-determined formula. The

system works on the premise that by linking a part of
earnings to productivity, the employees will respond by
increasing their labor productivity.

The gain-sharing component of an employee's
compensation is paid in the form of a bonus and
therefore demonstrates a direct linkage between the
employee's performance and the compensation earned.

Profit Sharing

These compensation systems are not related to an
individual's performance, but are linked to the profits
of an enterprise. The direct relationship between
individual performance and company performance is
less obvious but the aim is usually to demonstrate the

power of teamwork within the company. Here again, the profit is split with employees according to some predetermined formula.

Long-Term Incentives

Long-term incentive plans are operated, especially for executives, both as an incentive to improved performance and in order to reduce fixed costs. Examples of such schemes are:

- Share option plans to promote convergence of stockholder/executive interests.

- Bonus pay linked to long term performance (3–5 years) to encourage a focus on long-term goals.

These incentives are quite common in large, publicly owned corporations and can result in enormous take-home earnings when executives decide to cash in. When money is a strong motivator for an individual, these programs can be quite effective and they are economically sound, especially when an industry is experiencing a downturn.

Performance Bonus

This type of bonus can be based on individual or group

performance. Where it is individual based, the payment depends on performance ratings, and group-based bonuses are dependent upon team performance ratings. The overall management of this type of bonus system is extremely important as there is ample room for claims of favoritism due to the subjectivity of the process.

Skill-Based Pay

Skill-based pay refers to a pay system in which pay increases are linked to the number or depth of skills an employee acquires and applies directly to his or her job. This method is used as a means of developing broader and deeper skills among the workforce. Such increases are given in addition to, and not in lieu of, general pay increases employees may receive. The pay increases are usually tied to three types of skills:

1. Horizontal skills, which involve a broadening of skills in terms of the range of tasks.

2. Vertical skills, which involve acquiring skills of a higher level.

3. Depth skills, which involve a high level of skills in specialized areas relating to the same job.

Skill-based pay rewards a person for what he or she is worth to the organization, not what his or her job is worth to the organization. It takes into consideration that each employee brings a different set of skills, knowledge and aptitudes to a position and, therefore; the total contribution to the organization will change depending on who is doing what. This system rewards a broad range of skills, which encourages flexibility, skill development and continuous learning.

Self-Directed Work Teams

A self-directed work team is a group of people who combine different skills and talents to work toward a common purpose or goal. Members of a self-directed work team are involved on a routine basis in decision making, goal setting, scheduling, hiring, planning, peer review and problem solving. They use their company's mission statement to develop their purpose and direct their activity. Because a manager or boss does not lead, they must agree on the rules and deadlines for accomplishing what they set out to do. Many do this through the creation of a charter. If problems arise during the course of a project, the team members work together to provide a solution.

The role of managers and supervisors within organizations that support self-directed work teams is to help develop the team's self-directive capabilities. Rather than control and direct, the supervisors facilitate skill development. They also manage the interactions with and between other self-directed work teams in the organization.

The notion behind self-directed work teams is that maximizing employees' capabilities to contribute to organizational performance fosters an extremely high level of employee commitment. It is also linked to efforts to improve leadership and management skills among all employees.

All of these management methods have distinct merits and deserve careful consideration within organizations today. The issue at the heart of creating motivation-rich workplaces is that none of these methods alone or in combination will motivate all employees at all times. You can experiment with any or all of these methods, and you will find that some managers respond well to some systems as do the employees themselves, but it is only when you view the management method as one aspect of employee motivation that you will truly see an improvement in what we deem positive employee motivation levels.

THE MANAGEMENT

As we have been discussing throughout this book, different people have different internal motivating factors that influence how they react to the work they do. The internal motivators operating within an organization's managers have as great an affect on productivity as what is influencing their subordinate's behavior. It's the manager who has the greatest influence on employee behavior, and if the manager is not "buying into" the management method of the day, then he or she will be ineffective in using and applying the principles needed for the best outcome.

Every manager comes to his or her job with strongly held beliefs, values and motivating principles. If the management method espoused by the organization is not congruent with those beliefs, values and principles, then the manager suffers an internal conflict. He or she has to fight against their natural tendencies and ascribe to a way of dealing with people, directing work, making decisions, etc., that just doesn't fit. When the policies and managerial practices of an organization are out of synch with the managerial beliefs of the supervising person, then effective performance in his or her department is threatened.

When productivity, morale or other issues surface within that manager's department, the traditional answer to the problem is to send the manager on a training course. The thought is that by further educating the manager on the tools and techniques specific to a particular management method, the manager will change management behavior and beliefs. This indoctrination, so to speak, is often less than satisfactory, and while the manager may show some "improvement" in the short term, his or her natural style will eventually creep back in.

The whole notion of fitting a manager to a method rather than finding a method that fits the manager is flawed. This solution is based on the erroneous belief that there is one best way to manage people and that the "best" way just happens to be the management method being used currently. I'm hoping you're now beginning to agree that this is an ineffective premise to base a solution upon.

Trying to fit a manager to a certain mold is often like trying to fit a square peg into a round hole: It causes

frustration for the person trying to make the fit and severe discomfort for the person trying to be fit.

When organizations encourage and facilitate incongruence between a manager and the method under which that manager must manage, the resulting performance is mediocre at best and a dismal failure at worst. The repercussions of ineffective management are then felt throughout the department and organization as employees are left without effective leadership, direction and support.

THE MANAGED

Following the same arguments as above, when the practices of management are out of synch with the way the managed person wants to be supervised, then the performance of the supervised person suffers. Here, again, we are talking about the fact that not all people will respond positively to one particular method of management. Some employees will look at participative management as an ideal way to grow professionally and contribute meaningfully to the organization as a whole. Others will see it as demanding and invasive—requiring them to act outside their comfort zone. Those espousing participative management will respond that pushing people to explore their potential is a good thing and that both the organization and individual will benefit in the long run. This is a noble undertaking, but what effect does it have on the employee being forced to behave in a way that is unnatural and unwelcome? It will definitely cause undue stress and discomfort; two major contributing  factors to employee dissatisfaction. The end result is an employee who is unlikely to be motivated to do what the organization expects and his subsequent performance plummets.

Approaching motivational strategies with a one-prescription approach ignores the internal motivation factors that operate differently within each person. In order to develop a motivation-rich environment, you must consider each individual and the ways in which each person responds to motivating stimuli.

THE WORK

The final factor that needs to be considered when designing a motivation-rich work environment is the actual work that needs to be done within the organization. When the methods for managing are incongruent with the work to be done, then the performance of the work is negatively affected. When the work is highly structured and routinized, adding complicated layers of management hampers rather than helps productivity. When you don't require a team of people to decide how best to screw in a light bulb, don't use one. When a job can be redesigned for maximum satisfaction, then consider the possibility.

The point here is that just as there is no one "right" way to manage, neither is there one right way to organize jobs. The emphasis is, again, on making the job fit the people and the managerial techniques. Job design is a complicated subject but it deserves some attention within the context of this motivation book. The following is a summary of one technique you can apply within your organization. This introduction will give you some basic tools and the confidence you need to begin looking at the work structures you currently use.

The Job Characteristics Model

When we talk about the work that is done within organizations, there is a very useful framework that allows us to analyze and design jobs. It's called the Job Characteristics Model, and by using the model any job can be described in terms of the following five core job dimensions:

1. **Skill variety:** the degree to which a job requires a variety of different activities so the worker can use a number of different skills and talents.

2. **Task identity:** the degree to which the job requires completion of a whole and identifiable piece of work.

3. **Task significance:** the degree to which the job has a substantial impact on the lives or work of other people.

4. **Autonomy:** the degree to which the job provides substantial freedom, independence and discretion to the individuals in scheduling work and in determining the procedures to be used in carrying out the tasks.

5. **Feedback:** the degree to which carrying out the work activities required by the job results

in the individual obtaining direct and clear information about the effectiveness of his or her performance.

The first three dimensions—skill variety, task identity and task significance—combine to create meaningful work. That is, if these three characteristics exist in a job, we can predict that the person will view the job as being important, valuable and worthwhile. A job that allows autonomy gives the worker a sense of personal responsibility for the results, and if the job provides feedback, the employee will know how effectively he or she is performing. From a motivational standpoint, the Job Characteristics Model says that internal rewards are obtained by an employee when that person knows he or she personally has performed well on a task that he or she cares about.

Jobs high in motivating potential must be high in at least one of the three factors that lead to experiencing meaningfulness, plus they must be high on both autonomy and feedback. If jobs score high on motivating potential, the Job Characteristics Model predicts that motivation, performance and satisfaction will be positively affected, while the likelihood of absence and turnover is lessened. What managers can learn from the Job Characteristics Model are specific ways to make changes to jobs that are most likely to increase the motivational factors within each job.

- **Combine tasks.** Wherever possible, managers should take tasks that were split apart in the name of efficiency and put them back together to form new, larger modules of work that will increase skill variety and task identity.

- **Create natural work units.** The creation of natural work units means the tasks an employee does form an identifiable and meaningful whole. This increases employee ownership of the work and improves the likelihood that employees will view their work as meaningful and important rather than as irrelevant and boring.

- **Establish client relationships.** The client is the end user of the product or service the employee works on. Wherever possible, the manager should try to establish direct relationships between workers and their clients. This will increase skill variety, autonomy and feedback opportunities for the employee. The opportunity for increased awareness of the impact of one's work on others is a powerful motivator.

- **Expand jobs vertically.** Vertical expansion gives

employees responsibilities and controls that were formally reserved for management. It seeks to partially close the gap between the doing and the controlling aspects of the job and increases employee autonomy.

- **Open feedback channels.** By increasing feedback, employees not only learn how well they are performing their jobs, but also whether their performance is improving, deteriorating or remaining at a constant level. Ideally, this feedback about performance should be received directly as the employee does the job rather than from management on an occasional or even periodic basis.

The Job Characteristics Model is one way to determine the type of intrinsic motivational factors contained within a job. When discussing the type of work an employee is doing, it is a valuable exercise to examine ways in which the work can be reorganized to suit individual needs and desires.

The way work is managed is an important factor for employee success, and you want to make the process as simple and straightforward as possible. The more hoops that people need to jump through, the more opportunity for dissatisfaction; and the less satisfied employees are, the less motivated they are to do a good job. It is imperative that you not choose management systems simply because they are considered the latest and greatest. Just as certain management systems work for certain people, so do some systems work for some types of work and not for others.

The only way to achieve an environment that motivates all employees in the direction your organization desires is to align the four factors we have been discussing:

- Management Method

- The Manager

- The Managed

- The Work

Without congruity within these subsystems, you will never have a workplace that is totally dedicated to meeting your organizational needs and working at peak performance levels.

CREATING WORKPLACE CONGRUENCE FOR A MOTIVATION-RICH ENVIRONMENT

I don't think anybody yet has invented a pasttime that's as much fun, or keeps you as young, as a good job.

FREDRICK HUDSON ECKER, CHAIRMAN, METROPOLITAN LIFE

Based on the concept of the four interrelated work factors and our discussion about how these factors influence the way a workplace needs to be managed, we can develop four rules for workplace organization.

1. Different work must be organized in different ways.

2. The natural, personal style of the manager must fit with the work being done and the people who are doing the work.

3. Employees' values, beliefs and principles must be compatible with the way they are being managed and the work they are doing.

4. The particular managerial principles utilized by the manager must fit with the work to be done, the person doing the work, and the manager's style of managing.

Following these four rules creates a large degree of complexity within workplaces, but humans are complex beings and there are no short-cuts, especially when in comes to optimizing motivation and performance. It really is not as difficult as it appears. The key is to commit yourself to the premise that there is no one "right" way to manage. Once you remove this main obstacle, you will begin to see all of the employees within your organization as unique individuals who bring their own capabilities, values and beliefs to the workplace. When you recognize that none of these people is unmotivated or "wrong," you will be able to tackle the issue of employee motivation from an individual perspective, and this is when your workplace transformation will take place.

> *"You can buy a person's hands but you can't buy his heart. His heart is where his enthusiasm, his loyalty is."*
>
> STEPHEN COVEY

Example of Workplace Congruence in Action

Keys Manufacturing produces Hoozits. The process to produce a Hoozit involves fabricating and combining three different parts: the wheely, the rotator and the pin. Keys Manufacturing has three separate production departments each headed by a manager, and these managers all have different natural management styles. Bob, who is in charge of the fabrication of wheelies, is an authoritative manager who has been with the company for 20 years and runs a tight ship. Fred is in charge of producing the rotators and affixing the pins in preparation for the final assembly process. Fred is a new graduate from a progressive business school and he is very into the team approach and equality management. Gayle, the manager of the third production department, oversees the final assembly of the wheely to the rotator and pin combination. Gayle is a real "people person" who likes to foster personal relationships with her employees and has been working at Keys Manufacturing for five years.

Keys Manufacturing has been struggling with poor productivity and what seems to be a low level of motivation within the three production departments for the last two quarters—from around the same time that Fred joined the management team. Prior to Fred's arrival, there were only two production departments and productivity was high but it was hampered by an inefficient system.

That is what prompted the decision to split production into three stages and hire a third manager.

When Taylor, the Operations Manager, assessed the situation, he applied the principles for creating a congruent workforce and realized that after the reshuffle, each manager had people under them who were operating under three different behavioral and belief systems. Before the shuffle, most of the employee/manager incongruence had been attended to, but in the name of efficiency, those changes were discarded and staff members were assigned to a department based on skill set and experience alone.

What Taylor did to address the problem was reorganize the departments based on the kind of work being done and the suitability of the manager's natural style to the management style an employee responded to best. Then within each department the manager assigned duties based on each employee's preferences, natural ability and aptitude. The process was time consuming and the restructure caused an initial productivity decrease due to retraining requirements, but within three months the morale, satisfaction and productivity has climbed to levels that exceeded everyone's expectations. The managers were able to lead effectively using techniques that came naturally to them and that were intuitive and the employees were performing work and being managed in ways that best suited them.

This very simplified example gives you an idea of what it means to reorganize an entire workplace based on the four rules of workplace congruence. Of course, in the real world the solutions will not be so neat and straightforward, but the end rewards should be as significant. I didn't say it was easy, but with the right motivation and commitment on your part, it is doable.

To accomplish the task of creating a congruent workplace means putting employees' needs first. It also necessitates getting to know your employees and developing a true understanding of what makes them tick. It's not enough to know that Joe works in Accounting; you need to take the time to know what makes Joe in Accounting unique, what he values, what he likes about his job, what he dislikes about his job, and what he believes is an effective management system. Once you have the answers to these questions and many more, you will know how the company can bring out the best in him, and then it is your responsibility to make that happen.

The process of creating workplace congruence starts with open communication and includes systems that allow every employee to indicate the kind of work they are comfortable with, the type of management style they prefer, and one where managers can indicate their natural management-style preferences.

"Everything that can be counted does not necessarily count; everything that counts cannot necessarily be counted."

ALBERT EINSTEN

Create Congruence Through Recruitment and Selection

The most practical approach to creating congruence within your company is to develop hiring criteria based on the four factors required for workplace congruence. In other words, hire for cultural fit. Your culture is the outward manifestation of your corporate values, beliefs and principles, and the leaders, managers and supervisors within your organization most often represent this culture. The employees you bring into your business must support and nurture that culture, and they do that by contributing positively to daily interactions and ultimately finding their own success and fulfillment. Within a culture that motivates you will find employees doing work they enjoy for bosses to whom they relate well.

When you start with the right employees in the right positions, you are proactively addressing the ultimate motivation question, "How Should Manager X Manage Employee Y to Do What? To determine if a job candidate can be effectively managed by Manager X to do whatever the position requires, you need to take the time to find out who your candidates really are. You have to get beyond the education and experiences listed on their résumé and find out what brings out the best in that person. Ask questions in the interview process that address the "fit" factor and that reveal important information related to motivation, preferences, beliefs and values. Here are some questions to use as guidelines:

1. Tell me about the best boss you ever worked for. What made the relationship effective?

2. Tell me about a time when you were most dissatisfied working with a manager. What exactly caused the dissatisfaction?

3. Recall for me a time when you found it very difficult to get along with a coworker. What was the root of the problem?

4. If you could create the ideal work environment, what would it be like?

5. When were you most satisfied with your work performance?

6. What is the best thing a boss has ever said to you?

7. Tell me about a time when you were unmotivated and someone at your workplace was able to help you out of your slump. What did he or she do or say?

8. What is the most discouraging thing a boss has ever done or said to you? Why?

9. What is the best reward you have ever received at work?

10. What do you know about our company that excites you?

As you can see, all of these questions are designed to get the candidate thinking and talking about what is important to them and what makes a constructive, positive work environment. Answers to culture questions are not right or wrong: they simply are what they are. Your job is to evaluate how well your current environment, the work you offer, and the style of the management available will motivate the candidate to do a good, if not exceptional, job.

As we have been discussing, it is difficult for people to fight against their personality and natural inclinations and it is next to impossible to mold someone to fit into a situation where their values and principles are not in line with the environment. Start your employees off on a positive motivational track by making selection choices that enhance their natural motivation; you will be much more satisfied and so will your employees.

Congruence Through Planned Job Placement

This method uses techniques described in the workplace congruence example and is the one that organizations with existing motivation and performance issues will need to apply. The process is similar to recruitment where you are starting from scratch with current employees to determine where, within your company, each employee will get the most out of the work relationship.

You can accomplish this through informal meetings and conversations with staff, survey and questionnaires that you design yourself, or there are a wide variety of tests available which are designed to uncover personality, interests, aptitudes and management-style preferences. The following are sample questionnaires you can use with your employees to uncover their underlying motivational factors, their current motivation level, and how they approach motivating others.

SAMPLE MOTIVATION AND PERFORMANCE QUESTIONNAIRES

MOTIVATIONAL FACTO

Motivational Factors Questionnaire
GENERAL INSTRUCTIONS **Answer honestly:** There are no right or wrong answers. Your answers reflect your individuality and that is what we are trying to uncover. **Be specific:** When asked for examples, please provide as much detail as possible. The more we know about your unique set of skills, values and preferences, the higher the chance for a successful match. **Be introspective:** Take your time to answer the questions from your core beliefs, values, ideals, principles, etc. The more in-tune you are with what you truly desire from work, the better we are able to provide a fulfilling work environment. *Remember, this is not a test—there is no pass or fail. This is simply the best way for us to determine "fit."*

1.	When people meet you for the first time, what about their first impression is most inaccurate? (*Uncovers what the person values versus what they believe society values. The incongruence is important in that you get insight into how they might "try" to behave or come across vs. how they will truly perform.*)

Motivational Factors Questionnaire	
2.	Describe the workplace where you achieved the most satisfaction. Discuss specifically what makes that workplace stand out from the rest.
3.	Describe the workplace where you were the least satisfied. Discuss specifically the cause of your dissatisfaction.
4.	If you could create the ideal workplace, what would it look like?
5.	What has been your greatest work-related achievement? Please provide details about the job and the workplace where this achievement occurred. (*You're looking for a link between high performance and work environment—the ideal answer is one that occurred at the workplace described in question #2.*)
6.	Your ideal work hours are: ☐ Monday to Friday, 9–5 ☐ Flexible work time, 8-hour days ☐ No rules, I have a job to do and I take as many hours as needed to do it. ☐ Other: _____

Motivational Factors Questionnaire

7.	Your ideal remuneration is: ☐ Hourly pay ☐ Fixed salary ☐ Salary with a performance component ☐ Complete performance-based pay
8.	What is your expectation for yearly earnings? ☐ < $30,000 ☐ $30K–$50K ☐ $50K–$75K ☐ >$75K ☐ Money is not an expectation for me
9.	What is the best reward (monetary or otherwise) you have ever received at work? What made it so valuable to you?

Questions 10 to 16 are interrelated, please answer as such.

10.	If you had no limitations (geographical, type of industry, remuneration, etc.), what organization would you work for?
11.	Again, with no limitations (education, experience, specific skills), what function would you be performing in that organization?

	Motivational Factors Questionnaire
12.	In that function, what are the key responsibilities you would have?
13.	What are the main differences between that "ideal" role and the role you currently fulfill in your organization? (Looking for major differences between experience and desire—indicates where true passion lies.)
14.	What is holding you back from pursuing/getting your ideal role?
15.	Given what you know about our company, what is your ideal role here?
16.	What job title would best describe your ideal role? (Looking for creativity and unconventionality.)
17.	With what type of people do you prefer to work?
18.	Tell me about the most difficult coworker you ever worked with. What about the situation was most frustrating and what was the outcome?

Motivational Factors Questionnaire

19.	When making a decision, you:
	☐ Go with your gut.
	☐ Observe what has been done in the past, what was considered right.
	☐ Make quick decisions that deal with the here and now.
	☐ Consult superiors for their advice and guidance.
	☐ Look toward the future and strategize.
	☐ Involve many others and seek consensus/ cooperation.
	☐ Integrate many perspectives and stretch your thinking.
	☐ Examine how others would make the decision and decide based on a holistic view of the world.

Motivational Factors Questionnaire

20.	You work because: ☐ You need to earn a living. ☐ Work provides comfort and security. ☐ You need to be doing something. ☐ That is what responsible adults do. ☐ You are achievement and success oriented. ☐ You desire to make a positive contribution to the world. ☐ You value continual learning and self-improvement. ☐ You want to change the world.
21.	With which of the following people would you most want to work? ☐ Someone with the same background and same outlook on life. ☐ Someone with different experiences who has come to see the world the way you see it. ☐ Someone who is open to new ideas. ☐ Someone who sees the world totally different than you. ☐ Someone who has an entirely different cultural background.

Motivational Factors Questionnaire

22.	With which of the following people would you least want to work?

☐ Someone with the same background and same outlook on life.

☐ Someone with different experiences who has come to see the world the way you see it.

☐ Someone who promotes new ideas.

☐ Someone who sees the world totally different than you.

☐ Someone who has an entirely different cultural background.

Motivational Factors Questionnaire

23.	What is your perspective on a hierarchical work structure?

    ☐   It indicates your value within the company.

    ☐   That is how work evolved and it seems to be working.

    ☐   It is the often the only way to see to it that people do what they are supposed to do.

    ☐   I appreciate having superiors; I like order and structure.

    ☐   It is an efficient way to define strategies, determine what needs to be done, and achieve goals.

    ☐   It impedes effective communication within the organization.

    ☐   It places people into limiting roles, hampers full development.

    ☐   It is completely unnecessary; organizations consist of people already working toward a common goal so they don't need any limiting forces.

24.	What about our company excites you?

_____

_____

_____

_____

Current Motivation and Performance

Assessing Performance and Motivating Others

To find out how well you assess performance and motivate others, compare your total score to the following data (maximum score 120).

>101 . . . . top quartile

94–100. . . second quartile

85–93 . . . third quartile

< 84 . . . . . bottom quartile

When you gather information from all of your employees regarding their beliefs, practices, aptitudes and interests, you can begin the process of matching and work reorganization where necessary. Use the answers to the survey questions or the test results to begin a dialogue with your employees and to discover more about each one as an individual. This depth of knowledge and understanding will assist immeasurably in creating a congruent workplace and facilitating a motivation-rich work environment for everyone.

Ineffective performance arises when we don't know how Manager X should lead Employee Y to do what.

The most effective and thorough way to address that fundamental motivation question is through creating congruence between the four factors that lead to employee satisfaction and success: management methods, the manager, the managed and the work. When problems of performance, hence motivation, arise, they can often be attributed to the fact that in any organization, in any department, we find work requiring a basic kind of producer being done by people with many different beliefs and values who want to be managed in ways different than is the natural style of the manager.

Extensive evaluation and analysis of each employee's needs and desires and internal motivators is the key to discovering how best to use the talent you currently employ so that they can all be engaged in meaningful and satisfying work. The end result of a workplace full of satisfied and fulfilled employees is an environment where motivation flourishes, productivity is at or near capacity, and organizational success is optimized.

It sounds a bit utopian, but if you apply the principles discussed, you are well on your way to establishing a motivation-rich workplace that capitalizes on employees' natural internal motivators and encourages high participation and productivity.

Now that you have a solid grasp on how to build a motivation-rich foundation, we need to discuss the next steps in sustaining a motivation-rich environment over the long term. As you know now, employee motivation is subject to continual change, and, therefore, your work with motivation is one that requires diligent effort on a continual basis. To build a strong motivation culture, you need to commit to reevaluating your efforts and building processes that are inherently motivating to all of your employees.

The main factor in a sustainable, motivating workplace is employee recognition. And not gimmicky or showy recognition but true appreciation and gratitude for a job well done. You may think you have a great recognition program in place or that you recognize employees' efforts already, but please read the next chapter and think critically about what it is you recognize, how you recognize it, and how it is truly perceived by others within your organization.

motivation

"What you do speaks so loud that I cannot hear what you say."

RALPH WALDO EMERSON

chapter 3

RECOGNITION – THE KEY TO SUSTAINABLE MOTIVATION

"Recognition is critical in motivating, satisfying and retaining employees."

Praise and recognition are essential building blocks of a great workplace. All people possess the need to be recognized as individuals and to feel a sense of accomplishment. Recognition is an external motivator that applies to everyone and, therefore, it is relevant to our discussion of how to build a motivation-rich work environment. While there is nothing complicated about recognition, it is one of the items that most employees cite as missing from their workplaces.

A prevalent attitude in today's society is the notion that in order to do a good job and achieve our work-related goals, we must be very task and goal oriented. At work, the high (even medium) achievers seem so driven and focused—they are rushing here and rushing there, tending to issues, putting out fires, fielding requests: the priority is anything that is directly related to task achievement. When this occurs, what tends to happen is that people at work forget that there are lots of other people at work and that relationships with those people are a necessary component for success.

What I have been trying to emphasize throughout this book is the individuality and uniqueness of people in workplaces, and when you lose sight of the people factor, you lose the ability to relate effectively with employees and coworkers. On the other hand, when you establish real relationships with people, you desire to know what excites them, what interests them, what guides them, and what motivates them. And when you have real relationships with employees at work, you are necessarily appreciative of their contributions. When you see employees and coworkers as more than a means to accomplish work goals, you will treat them with the respect, trust and appreciation they desire. This is the frame of reference that forms the foundation for meaningful recognition.

"The word "appreciation" means to be thankful and express admiration, approval or gratitude. It also means to grow or appreciate in value. As you appreciate life, you become more valuable—both to

yourself and others."

SARA PADDISON, HIDDEN POWER OF THE HEART

Recognition isn't something you "do" like all the other tasks you have at work. Recognition is a mind-set; it is a way of relating to your employees on a daily basis. You are never "done" recognizing and it never gets checked off your to-do list. When you commit to recognition, you must commit to treating your employees as people. It's simple really, but it takes a reframing of the purpose of your interactions with everyone at work. Yes, you are at work to accomplish goals so you must direct and lead people, but because you need to get work done through and with people, you must also accept your responsibility for fulfilling people's affiliation needs at work.

The small interactions that occur on a regular basis are what make a real impact on employees. When you praise someone, when you hold team meetings, when you keep your staff informed about changes, when you express confidence in someone's ability, and even when you give someone a warm smile, you are using recognition. **You are communicating that you recognize the importance and value of others,** and therein lays the motivating power of recognition.

RECOGNITION—A WORTHY CHALLENGE

"Recognition is so easy to do and so inexpensive to distribute that there is simply no excuse for not doing it."

ROSABETH MOSS KANTER,
AUTHOR AND HARVARD BUSINESS SCHOOL PROFESSOR

One element common to all individuals is the need for reward and praise. It is something we work hard for and yet, all too often, our work goes unrecognized. We do a good job, we get results, but somehow we don't get thanked. Why is this? In too many cases the notion of recognition has been overanalyzed. We have made the process so complex and full of rules when in fact it is very simple.

- Thank employees for a job well done.

- Be appreciative.

- Acknowledge good work.

There is nothing more motivating than praise and recognition. At the root of every effective workplace performance program is a philosophy of recognizing and appreciating employees. To quote Bob Nelson, the motivation mastermind, "You get the best effort from others not by lighting a fire beneath them, but by building a fire within them." This is where the power of reward and recognition become so powerful and so undeniable. **By recognizing an employee's work, you are providing intrinsic motivation for him or her to do better and be better.**

> *"There is more hunger for love and appreciation in this world than for bread."*
>
> MOTHER TERESA

If you are still thinking of recognition as another complication to your already hectic job, think again. Recognition doesn't need to be time consuming or complex, and the results of meaningful recognition will significantly reduce the other stressors you have in your work life that are caused by dissatisfied employees.

With effective recognition you will find employees are more willing to get involved with problem solving and they will rely less on you to find the solutions. The more appreciated an employee feels, the more connected he or she feels to the work. This increased connectivity leads to increased pride and ownership and a desire to take on more responsibility. As employees are more committed to their work, they will show an increased concern for quality and company reputation. Their increased investment in the company is a direct result of meaningful recognition and they will naturally want to contribute more to the workplace even in the face of adversity.

If you are still in doubt, take a look at the results of a Recognition-Performance survey conducted by Bob Nelson, considered one of the leading experts on workplace motivation:

Statement	Agreement
"Recognizing employees helps me better motivate them."	90.5%
"Providing non-monetary recognition to my employees when they do good work helps to increase their performance."	84.4%
"Recognizing employees provides them with practical feedback."	84.4%
"Recognizing my employees for good work makes it easier to get the work done."	80.3%
"Recognizing employees helps them to be more productive."	77.7%

"Providing non-monetary recognition helps me to achieve my personal goals."	69.3%
"Providing non-monetary recognition helps me to achieve my job goals."	60.3%

- 72.9% of managers reported that they received the results they expected when they used recognition either immediately or soon after the event being recognized occurred.

- 98.8% of managers said they felt they would eventually obtain the desired results by using recognition.

- 77.6 % of the employees who worked for the managers participating in the survey said that it was very or extremely important to be recognized by their manager when they do good work.

- The time frame that these same employees expected recognition to occur after the event was:

— Immediately (20%)

— Soon thereafter (52.9%)

— Sometime later (18.8%)

These results support the dynamic and self-reinforcing effect of recognition in the workplace as follows:

1. A manager using recognition is reinforced by the impact that the recognition has on improving employee's job performance.

2. Improved employee performance in turn reinforces the manager to continue providing recognition.

Effective recognition breathes life into a workplace. It creates a dynamic exchange of ideas and it boosts morale, productivity, loyalty and motivation. These qualities will make your job as a manager much easier and you will wonder why you ever griped about having to recognize people in the first place.

"Generally, appreciation means some blend of thankfulness, admiration, approval and gratitude. In the financial world, something that "appreciates" grows in value. With the power

tool of appreciation, you get the benefit of both perspectives: as you learn to be consistently thankful and approving, your life will grow in value."

DOC CHILDRE AND HOWARD MARTIN,
HEARTMATH SOLUTION

Recognition That Motivates

"This business of making another person feel good in the unspectacular course of his/her daily comings and goings is, in my view, the very essence of leadership."

IRWIN FEDERMAN, CEO, MONOLITHIC MEMORIES, INC.

To understand the difference between recognition that works and recognition that doesn't, I want you to recall the story I related about my own experiences with workplace motivation and recognition at the beginning of this book. Remember, we had put in numerous programs designed to recognize and reward employees but none of them actually worked. Well, here are some comments from employees in other organizations that support why those programs were dismal failures:

- "Please, not another golf shirt!"

- "Why spend money on all these silly trinkets; put the money to use and buy us a photocopier that prints more than five pages a minute."

- "Think of the trees and time wasted printing those crazy certificates. What do we do with them? Take them home and display them on the fridge?"

- "If I have to spend another lunch hour listening to the employee-of-the-month speech, I'm gonna lose it."

- "Rather than go through some big hoopla, why not just tell us when we do something well?"

Do you recognize your own recognition efforts in any of those comments? It's easy to fall into the trap of meaningless recognition because meaningless recognition takes little to no personal involvement. The recognition programs alluded to in the above comments are all company sponsored. As a manager or supervisor, you don't really contribute anything to the process and you can sit back thinking your employees are taken care of and concentrate on the real work that needs to be done. The very items that we have been trained to consider as recognition have very little recognition value. We too often equate reward with recognition, and while the reward may be nice to have when its in the form of a raise, bonus, plaque or prize, it's the thought behind the reward that is the actual recognition and that is exactly what gets lost in the giving.

For rewards to count as recognition, employees need to see acknowledgment of their specific accomplishments and sincere appreciation for their personal value to the organization. Without that link, a reward is just another external motivator that may or may not have value to the individual receiving it. This doesn't mean, however, that there is no place for reward in the workplace. Rewards can be very motivating (providing it has value to the person receiving it), and it is important to think of new and creative ways to reward your employees. In fact, the second half of this book is dedicated to providing ideas for rewards that have worked for many employees. The point you need to remember is that the reward does not equal recognition.

You can make a reward a form of recognition, though, by delivering the reward in such a way that fosters recognition. Perks, incentives and bonuses themselves aren't recognition, but by personalizing them, the employee then perceives it as a form of recognition. Rather than handing out bonus checks with the regular payroll, meet employees and tell them how the company did, stress that everyone's hard work contributed to the prosperity, and that the company is appreciative of their efforts. When an incentive is earned, make sure you meet with the employee directly and discuss what he or she did that directly contributed to the receipt of the incentive. Do the same for perks, plaques and other rewards that are given periodically. The key is to tie the reward to employee performance and then express appreciation.

Six Factors of Effective Recognition

Effective recognition can be defined as, "Motivation that increases the self-esteem and initiative of the recipient, resulting in a lasting improvement in their behavior and performance which positively impacts the bottom line." When expressing appreciation and recognizing employees, you must take into consideration the following six basic factors of effective recognition:

Recognition that motivates is:

Genuine: It is not forced and it has no ulterior motive.

Spontaneous: It is not premeditated, planned or prepared.

Personal: It means something special to the person it is given to and he or she is singled out for praise.

Specific: It is more than "good job" or "way to go"; it's a "thank you" or acknowledgement for something specific that was done.

Timely: It comes as close to the event as possible—this reinforces spontaneity.

Public: Expressing thanks is generally not a "behind closed doors" event. Find ways to let everyone know how proud you are of the work that is being done. ***Note: For those individuals who you know are uncomfortable with high visibility, DO NOT publicly acknowledge—this will only end up embarrassing and de-motivating him or her.*

Not all six factors have to be present for recognition to be important, but you need to aim for as many as possible every time. The only exception is the notion of public praise—some people are very averse to publicity and the embarrassment of the situation will take away any recognition value. Remember, your goal is to relate to your employees in meaningful terms, and through your understanding and relationship with employees you will know whether public praise is appropriate or not. If you don't, then you need to re-read the beginning of this chapter and commit to getting to know your employees on a personal level.

- Recognition that works inspires the recognizee to say, "That made my day!"

- Recognition that works is memorable. It can be unique and creative but it doesn't have to be; it just has to make a lasting, positive impression upon the person receiving the recognition.

- Recognition that works is heartfelt. It can be elaborate but most often employees say it is the little things that mean the most.

- Recognition opportunities are everywhere. Employees are looking for proof that they are valued and appreciated in everything you do and everything you say. That means you have to make recognition an inherent part of your work environment. From the amount and type of information you communicate to the trust you demonstrate to the safety of your workplace, every opportunity for interaction with employees is an opportunity to convey appreciation and value.

Build a Recognition Culture

"Treating people with respect will gain one wide acceptance and improve the business."

TAO ZHU GONG
500 BC, ASSISTANT TO THE EMPEROR OF YUE

Recognition is easy, once you realize what it really entails, but it is not necessarily intuitive. This is why you must start building recognition into the culture of your organization. It is important that managers and supervisors understand the principles of recognition but it is equally important that all employees believe that recognition is part of the value system within the company. To evaluate the state of your current recognition culture, ask yourself the following questions:

1. Do your managers know how and why to recognize their employees?

   Evaluate both the incidences of managers who do not believe in recognition and therefore do not give any as well as those who give too much. A manager who does his or her best to motivate people, but "over-recognizes" by awarding everyone even when they don't deserve it is equally as ineffective at recognition as the manager who does nothing at all.

2. Do you offer recognition training?

   Recognition training is recommended for both
   new and experienced supervisors. Recognition
   is far too important to throw your dollars at the
   reward programs when your managers don't
   understand how and don't have the skill to
   recognize effectively.

3. Does your Human Resource Department
   conduct employee-recognition surveys?

   Communication and feedback are critical
   to developing and managing an effective
   recognition program. Asking employees what
   they want in their recognition program is
   one of the most important things the Human
   Resource Department can do when creating
   and managing a recognition program. Surveys,
   focus groups, forums, interviews, etc., are all
   effective means to solicit recognition feedback.
   Use the information as the primary source to
   learn what works well and what part of the
   program is ineffective so improvements can
   be implemented. A company-wide employee-
   recognition survey is recommended annually.
   The key is to ask the right questions and create a

base line so you can compare progress from one year to the next.

4. Do you have a communication process for employees to give feedback and share their thoughts and ideas about recognition throughout the year?

    Feedback can be done via suggestions boxes, Web sites, e-mail or even a recognition hotline number. The most important aspect of the feedback loop is to make sure that all suggestions are acknowledged and that good suggestions are acted upon. When employees see that their ideas are making a difference, they will share the good news with others, which will increase employee "buy in."

5. Do your recognition efforts go beyond those departments where quantitative, measurable results that directly impact the bottom line are obvious?

    Organizations are notorious for creating elaborate reward programs for employees in sales departments. These types of companies place high value on jobs that have a direct link to profits but that sends the message to all other employees that their contributions are subclass. Be sure that your reward criteria is inclusive so all employees can fairly participate in the program. You may have to create different reward and recognition criteria for different departments—the bottom line is, though, you need to make rewards attainable for everyone.

After you have evaluated the current state and determined if your recognition efforts are on target, way out in left field, or perhaps nonexistent, it is now time to make changes. You need to start at the top and make recognition a part of your corporate values. When you redefine your overall purpose to include valuing your employees and recognizing their accomplishments, you send a strong message to everyone within the company that people matter. Start today by recognizing your own employees and create a recognition buzz that transmits company wide.

Recognition Is Infectious

The leaders and managers within a company will be expected to champion recognition but individual employees are not exempt from the process. When employees begin to feel the difference that recognition makes in their work life, they will naturally try to pass on that feeling when dealing with coworkers of their own. The very act of recognizing someone creates a special feeling within ourselves as well. We know that we are making someone else feel valued and that makes us feel wonderful. The fallout of these warm, fuzzy feelings is very helpful in mitigating the everyday stressors people feel at work and can improve morale, motivation and productivity in and of itself.

Working in a cold and indifferent environment does nothing to improve burnout and a lack of enthusiasm, but working in a warm environment full of camaraderie and positive energy has the power to boost anyone out of a slump. You see, when you begin recognizing and valuing people, the response can only be positive, and even the most negative and jaded people have no choice but to be influenced. Deliberate recognition starts the process and pretty soon recognition becomes so intuitive that people don't even realize they are "recognizing" someone, they just know they are treating others with respect and appreciation—and that is precisely what this whole motivation discussion is all about. To motivate someone, you must first "get" that person, and when you get others, they get you and then they are that much more likely to work for and with you to accomplish whatever needs to be done.

Recognition is all about the human factor and that

means recognition can move upwards too! Don't forget to let your manager know that you appreciate him or her and the support he or she provides. Managers at all levels are bombarded with complaints and all the other unsavory stuff that comes with the job. A little genuine recognition thrown their way will increase the likelihood even more that he or she reciprocates with recognition of their own. Don't give recognition upwards in order to receive something as that is not genuine and will only get you labeled a brown-noser. Do give recognition up with no other intention but to make someone's day. Too often we take good management for granted when instead it should be shouted from the rooftops and held up for example.

A corporate culture that is strong in recognition is one where all employees flourish. Don't take anyone or anything for granted within your organization. Encourage people on a daily basis and watch them reach and strive for more and more fulfillment. Just as trying to answer the irrelevant question, "How do you motivate employees?" puts you in a vicious cycle of trying one motivation method after another, effective recognition creates a cycle of its own but it is a positive cycle that generates positive energy and yields continually greater positive results.

Deciding What to Reward/Recognize

When we talk about the power of recognition and reward, it is imperative that we remember the adage, "What gets rewarded or recognized gets done." Together these elements form a powerful motivational elixir, and when you begin to create a culture  that is based on appreciation and gratitude, employee performance in those areas you are rewarding and recognizing will improve. "What's the problem?" you ask. Well, there is no problem unless what you are rewarding and recognizing turns out not to be what you intended.

Does the complexity never end? Unfortunately it does not and, therefore, you need to manage your rewards and recognition to ensure the "right" behavior is being appreciated.

Right Behavior Turned Wrong

It is easy to inadvertently steer your employees to act in ways that on the surface appear great, but that actually breed inefficiency, complacency, dishonesty, and worse. Examples:

- If you begin informal or formal recognition for meeting budgets, you may encourage short-cuts within departments that are not in the company's best interest.

- Recognizing long-standing service may encourage mediocrity and not necessarily high performance.

- Recognizing low numbers of safety infractions might encourage the suppression of incidents, potentially increasing the chances of a major accident down the road.

- If you recognize sales leads rather than profitability, you end up encouraging quantity over quality and decreasing your competitiveness.

These are just a few examples of how well-meaning

recognition, done in very effective ways, can lead to ineffective and inappropriate personal, team and organization behavior. Before instituting any reward and/or recognition program, be diligent in defining exactly what you want to reward/recognize and why.

I know I just spent a whole section of this book telling you to recognize spontaneously and not overanalyze the process, but that applies to the *way* in which recognition is given not to *what* is actually recognized. Not every organization will want to recognize the same behavior. It is important that you spend sufficient time at the beginning to plan and prepare your recognition program. The best and most efficient method for doing this involves five steps:

1. Define Organizational Values and Goals

   A successful reward/recognition program is based primarily on an organization's goals and values. **What is the ultimate reason the organization exists and what does it hope to accomplish?** You need this information in order to determine what behaviors are most compatible with the organization's strategic goals because those are the behaviors you want to target for formal and informal recognition.

2. Benchmark Top Performance

In this step you identify current top performers and define what it is that they do that is exemplary, unique, compelling, etc. **What is it specifically that sets some employees apart from their peers?** These specific behaviors are then used as benchmarks for determining what you want to recognize, promote, and ultimately what you want to motivate others to do.

3. Define Your "Right" Behaviors

Now that you understand what your top performers are doing that is noteworthy, you need to analyze these behaviors and determine whether widespread, similar performance will help achieve organizational goals. It is at this point that you must identify potential negative repercussions of the behavior you are rewarding. **Is the behavior going to encourage short-term gain at the expense of long-term profitability, competitiveness or sustainability?** Put each behavior through a rigorous test to make sure it is compatible with why you are implementing the program in the first place.

4. Communicate Your Expectations

The next required component is to clearly define what you expect from all employees and then tell them. As with any change initiative, you must effectively communicate what you are trying to accomplish and why. With any reward and recognition, it is imperative that you go one step further and outline specifically what you expect from employees. This is no time to test how well your employees understand the organization's goals—you need to be clear and explicit when explaining what types of behaviors you want to promote. **What is it exactly that employees need to be doing on a consistent basis?** Communicate this to them and help them understand their role within the larger context of the organization as whole.

5. Set Up Employees for Success

The last and probably most critical component to consider when beginning to design a reward and recognition program is to catch employees doing things right. Provide lots of opportunity for informal recognition and make sure even the smallest efforts get recognized. **What are employees doing to head in the**

right direction? The reason for reward and recognition is to build intrinsic motivation, and remember, the most motivating thing for people is praise and appreciation. Start with the small changes or the everyday achievements and gradually build your expectations. You will find your employees' expectations of themselves will increase over time as well.

Reward and recognition itself is not complex but it is challenging. It challenges how appreciative you are of your employee's and coworker's efforts, it challenges how you interact with them, and it challenges how you define success. It is, however, a very worthy and important challenge; one that you should begin tackling today.

SETTING UP YOUR RECOGNITION PROGRAM

"Recognition is something a manager should be doing all the time--it's a running dialogue with people."

RON ZEMKE, SENIOR EDITOR, TRAINING MAGAZINE

Now that you are armed with lots of theory, in-depth understanding and practical solutions for employee recognition, it is time to build a recognition program that meets the needs of your organization. This process is best done with a three-stage approach:

1. Assess your current recognition efforts.

2. Identify and plan your recognition strategy.

3. Acknowledge that your recognition plan requires continuous evaluation.

Assess Your Current Recognition Efforts

When you are trying to assess your current recognition practices, you need to go directly to the source. This is not an exercise for you and or your management team, because you will almost certainly view your level of recognition and appreciation much differently than those on the receiving end. There are a number of reasons for the difference in perception—be assured the differences are there. Common problems related to ill-perceived recognition include the actual delivery of a recognition message, problems with what gets recognized in the workplace, the overall recognition culture, degree of communication, and fairness of the recognition. Any effort you make toward recognizing and outwardly appreciating your employees is to be commended, but you can't give yourself a whole-hearted pat on the back until you know what your employees think and say about your efforts when they talk among themselves or with friends and family.

In order to obtain a complete picture of your recognition efforts, it is also a good idea to assess employee satisfaction with the various factors that coincide with recognition and motivation in the workplace. For instance, you can't support a high-recognition culture if you don't communicate well with your employees. A workplace that doesn't encourage diverse expression of one's opinion is not likely to support and use recognition or motivational practices. A high-stress-inducing workplace will discourage motivational efforts of which recognition is one of the most important. It is more than just direct recognition activities that count, it is entire atmosphere, practices and workplace culture that need to be examined before embarking on a recognition program designed to improve or enhance positive employee motivation.

The best way to gather this type of information is with a cross-reference survey whereby you and other managers complete a recognition practices inventory and then have your employees fill out the same survey. What this process will reveal are the areas in which you are already doing a good job with recognition and areas where you are falling short. Perhaps what you, your colleagues and senior management consider appropriate and highly effective are not at all well received by your employees. Or maybe you think you are doing a good job of communicating with your employees when in fact their perception is much different. You need to uncover these inconsistencies and then develop a plan to remedy them in order to build a strong recognition culture and a highly motivated workplace.

The following is a survey example that you can use or adapt for your own purposes:

CURRENT RECOGNITION PRACTICES AND EMPLOYEE SATISFACTION SURVEY

Current Recognition Practices and Employee Satisfaction Survey
Answer the survey questions using the following scale: **Always   Frequently   Occasionally   Seldom   Never** **Recognition Activity**

1.	Employees are given verbal praise.
2.	Employees are given written praise (thank-you notes, cards, etc.).
3.	Employees are given praise through e-mail.
4.	Employees are given praise in public (at meetings, special events, informal groups, etc.).
5.	Employees are given certificates for specific accomplishments or achievements.

Current Recognition Practices and Employee Satisfaction Survey

6.	Employees are given small monetary rewards for achievement (gift certificates, coupons, dinner, flowers, etc.).
7.	Employees are rewarded with paid time off from work.
8.	Employees are offered flexible work schedules.
9.	Employees are offered choice of work/assignments where appropriate.

Recognition Effectiveness

10.	Employees are given recognition in a genuine manner.
11.	Employee recognition is given in a timely manner.
12.	Employees appreciate the type of recognition they receive.
13.	Attempts are made to individualize the recognition provided.
14.	Employees feel more valued after a recognition activity.
15.	Employees have equal opportunity to receive recognition within our organization.

Current Recognition Practices and Employee Satisfaction Survey

Feedback Activity

16.	Employees are given useful and constructive feedback.
17.	Employees are given adequate feedback about their performance.
18.	Employees receive feedback that helps them improve their performance.
19.	Employee feedback is given in a timely manner.
20.	Employees have an opportunity to participate in the goal-setting process.
21.	Employee performance evaluations are fair and appropriate.
22.	When employees do a good job, they receive the praise and recognition they deserve.

Degree of Teamwork

23.	Our organization practices and encourages teamwork.
24.	There is a strong feeling of teamwork and cooperation in our organization.

Current Recognition Practices and Employee Satisfaction Survey

Degree of Customer Focus

25.	Letters from customers are circulated or posted for all employees to see.
26.	Employees are held accountable for the quality of work they produce.
27.	Our organization maintains a very high standard of quality.
28.	Our organization understands its customers' needs.

Awareness of Mission and Purpose

29.	Employees have a good understanding of the mission and the goals of our organization.
30.	Employees understand how their work directly contributes to the overall success of our organization.
31.	Employees are provided with regular updates and information about the mission and the goals of our organization.
32.	Employees understand the organization's strategic goals.
33.	Employees derive personal satisfaction from achieving organization goals.

Current Recognition Practices and Employee Satisfaction Survey

Compensation

34.	Employees are paid fairly for the work they do.
35.	Employees' salaries are competitive with similar jobs.
36.	Employees' benefits are comparable to those offered by other organizations.
37.	Employees understand and use their benefit plan for optimum results.
38.	Employees are satisfied with their benefit package.

Workplace Resources

39.	Employees are given the resources required to do their job well.
40.	The requisite information systems are in place and accessible for employees to accomplish their tasks.
41.	The workplace is well maintained.
42.	The workplace is a physically comfortable place to work.
43.	The workplace is safe.

Current Recognition Practices and Employee Satisfaction Survey

Opportunities for Growth

44.	Employees are given adequate opportunities for professional growth in our organization.
45.	Employees receive the training they need to do their job well.
46.	Managers are actively involved in the professional development and advancement of their employees.
47.	Managers encourage and support employee development.
48.	Employees are encouraged to learn from their mistakes.
49.	Employees have mentors or coaches at work from whom they can learn.
50.	Employees consider their work challenging.
51.	Employees consider their work stimulating.
52.	Employees consider their work rewarding.

Work/Life Balance

53.	The environment in our organization supports a balance between work and personal life.
54.	Managers encourage employees to maintain a balance between work and personal life.

Current Recognition Practices and Employee Satisfaction Survey

55.	Employees are able to satisfy both their job and family responsibilities.
56.	Employees are provided a work pace that is conducive to good work.
57.	Employee workloads are reasonable.
58.	Expectations placed on employees are reasonable.
59.	Employees do not suffer unreasonable stress due to the functions of their jobs and their position within our organization.

Fairness and Consistency

60.	Employees are treated fairly within our organization.
61.	Policies are administered as consistently as possible within our organization.
62.	Employees are awarded raises, promotions, special assignments, etc., in accordance with stated policies.
63.	Favoritism or other workplace relationships are not used as factors when dealing with workplace issues.

Respect for Employees

64.	Employees are always treated with respect.
65.	Employees are listened to within our organization.

Current Recognition Practices and Employee Satisfaction Survey

66.	The culture of our organization fosters respect for employees.
67.	Employees' special skills, abilities and talents are valued within our organization.
68.	Managers and coworkers care about each other as people.

Communication

69.	Information and knowledge are shared openly within our organization.
70.	Communication is encouraged within our organization.
71.	Managers do a good job of sharing information.
72.	Senior management communicates well with the rest of the organization.

Personal Expression

73.	Employees are allowed to challenge or question current practices or decisions.
74.	Employees can disagree with their manager without fear of reprisal.
75.	Employees can express their opinions openly at work.

Current Recognition Practices and Employee Satisfaction Survey	
76.	Employees in our organization have diverse backgrounds.

As you can see from the questions in the survey, what you are trying to assess is the overall morale and satisfaction within the workplace. By comparing managers' responses to those of employees', it will become apparent where there are issues of conflict. Make detailed notes of these areas of concern and refer to them constantly as you begin to plan and execute recognition guidelines that will work for your company and your employees.

You may even want to go one step further with each conflict area and gather more in-depth information about the issues that are most concerning for employees. Any steps you can take to make your workplace more open and communicative, the better managers and employees will get along and respect each other—two of the most important ingredients for a high-motivation workplace in the first place.

Identify and Plan Your Recognition Strategy

Now that you have a good understanding and awareness of your current recognition practices

and overall employee satisfaction, you are ready
to formulate a plan for establishing an effective
recognition strategy. Armed with the information you
gathered that indicates where you are doing a good job
and what areas need improvement, you can begin to set
out recognition guidelines that will encourage the type
of behavior and activity your organization desires and
hopefully eliminate negative and detracting behaviors.

> **Before embarking on this next step, remember
> to keep in mind the basic rule of motivation:**
> *Different people are motivated by different things
> at different times.*

The impact of this rule is significant because it
means that your job is not to create a one-size-fits-all
recognition program but rather to set out guidelines for
recognition that have enough flexibility and creativity
so as to accommodate all the users and recipients. To
accomplish this multi-variant task you will need to
be quite organized, and the best way to approach the
process is with a structured plan. I've outlined what
I feel are the basic steps required in such a plan, and
you can modify them according to how your company
generally undertakes any change initiative.

STEP 1: Form a Recognition Program
Development Committee

When you develop a recognition program, it is beneficial to have a committee or other type of team assist you with the overall program development and management. The program will be for everyone and, therefore, it is important that there be a broad representation of ideas from within the company. Managers and employees should share jointly in the development and administration of the program to ensure that the interests and preferences of all groups are represented and incorporated appropriately. The committee will determine the general direction of the recognition efforts and will manage the communication and feedback process once the program begins.

This recognition program development committee will assist with program management and development in the following ways:

- Publicize the program.

- Conduct and administer feedback information solicited during the process.

- Determine overall recognition guidelines including formal and informal recognition efforts.

- Suggest recognition program components as well as various rewards or activities that are inline with the overall values and principles within your organization.

- Provide rewards and make arrangements for special events that pertain to or support employee recognition activity.

Being part of this recognition committee can also be used as a powerful tool in employee recognition and appreciation. Many employees are motivated by increased responsibility or new tasks, and the opportunity to participate on the committee can be an incentive or perk for the right employee. What you want to avoid is any perception of favoritism, so make sure whatever process you use is transparent and gives equal opportunity to all who would express a desire to be a part of the process. Other factors to consider for committee membership include:

- Length of term for committee members.

- A process for membership that ensures at least one experienced member remains on the committee. This provides for continuity and consistency.

- Who is tasked with overall responsibility for the committee.

- How committee membership is actually attained (election, appointment, volunteer, etc.).

STEP 2: Conduct an Employee Opinion Survey

I know there have been a lot of surveys suggested for you to perform as you venture along this path to create a high-motivation workplace. I can't emphasize enough, however, the importance of getting feedback and input from employees—it is the only way you will learn what is most valuable to them, and without individual value, your recognition and motivation efforts will be lackluster at best. In order for your recognition committee to develop an effective recognition strategy, you must go to the source and find out what types of recognition will meets the needs, expectations and preferences of your employees. The easiest and most efficient way to do this is through a survey. I have created an example below, but please use your imagination and creativity, and hopefully some specific ideas from the second half of this book, to construct your own survey.

EMPLOYEE RECOGNITION SURVEY

Employee Recognition Survey
People are individuals and, as such, everyone has their own unique preference for being recognized. Because everyone's needs are different, we would like you to fill out the following survey to give us an indication of the type of recognition you value and what you would consider a motivator. Additionally, we would like to know what you would like to do to help us create a supportive and appreciative workplace where everyone feels respected and valued. Responses will be shared with your immediate supervisor or manager only. *I prefer to be recognized by (check all that apply):*
☐   Public praise.
☐   Praise given privately in person.
☐   Note of thanks.

Employee Recognition Survey

☐ Letter of commendation for personnel file, copy to unit/department head.

☐ E-mail message to unit.

☐ Personal e-mail.

☐ Mention in newsletter or on Web site.

☐ A small personalized gift; e.g., coffee mug, plaque, certificate.

☐ Food items.

☐ Gift certificates.

☐ Formal recognition programs and ceremonies (employee of the month, year).

☐ Opportunity to attend training of choice.

☐ Opportunity to participate on committees and task forces.

☐ Opportunity to work on teams or with others.

☐ Have lunch with supervisor.

☐ Nomination for specific awards for process improvement, customer service, safety, attendance, cost-saving ideas, etc.

Employee Recognition Survey

☐ Other, please describe: _____

_____

_____

_____

_____

☐ I would enjoy participating in a recognition program that helps me recognize my coworkers' efforts.

☐ I am willing to serve on a unit committee to develop and maintain recognition in our workplace.

Please list other ways to show general appreciation to all employees and coworkers: _____

_____

_____

_____

_____

Thank you for your input.

Conducting an employee opinion survey can assist a recognition committee in identifying preferred types of awards, establishing nomination and selection procedures and determining the frequency and method(s) of award presentation preferred by employees.

STEP 3: Identify Your Recognition Program Purpose

Once you have begun laying the groundwork for a recognition program (developed the committee, surveyed employees, analyzed survey results), you need to create a mission statement for your committee to follow. As you have been discovering throughout this book, motivation and recognition are highly subjective processes that can be misrepresented, misunderstood and misapplied very easily. Your committee members will need a clear and focused mission to guide them when making decisions regarding the recognition guidelines, practices and programs that are most appropriate for your company and its employees.

Some factors to consider when developing your recognition program's mission include:

- Tailor the program to suit the needs of employees and to complement the type(s) of work done in each department/unit/facility/etc.

- Make a clear link between the recognition program's mission and that of the organization and its individual departments.

- Remember that what gets rewarded or

recognized gets done. Emphasize core skills and functions by incorporating them into the recognition or reward initiatives.

- The mission must support the goal of any recognition program which is to provide a program that is fair and flexible, that meets the needs of employees, and provides an opportunity to formally recognize and reward their efforts and accomplishments.

- Ensure the mission includes both formal and informal recognition practices.

STEP 4: Define Recognition Themes and Criteria

Identifying themes and criteria for achievement and formal recognition are necessary so that employees understand why an award has been given. It also helps them to determine what they can do to earn recognition for their own efforts. Make sure you communicate your intentions and the rationale for the criteria—this encourages buy-in and also helps employees understand your mission. Some recognition themes that you may want consider are as follows:

- Overall excellence

- Attendance

- Customer service

- Distinguished service

- Teamwork

- Technical achievement

- Creativity or innovation

- Leadership

- Commitment and dedication

- Above and beyond a job description

- Flexibility or adaptability to change

- Employee/team player of the month/quarter/period/year

- Money-saving suggestion award

- Personal achievement award

- Educational achievement

- Community service

- Workplace safety award

- Morale booster

- Most fun

- Professional development

- Skill improvement

STEP 5: Recognition Eligibility Factors

After the recognition theme(s) have been chosen, the recognition committee needs to set in place a process for both informal and formal recognition to take place. Key components to setting up a successful recognition program are fairness, consistency and an equal chance for reward. This process will take much communication between the committee, senior management and department managers, and it requires extensive communication with employees. The slightest hint of bias in the recognition eligibility can derail your whole process and make it that much more difficult to introduce modifications. The end result will be more de-motivation than you had in the first place.

Questions to consider when developing eligibility requirements are as follows:

Informal Recognition

- Do the managers and supervisors have the tools required to feel comfortable with informal recognition?

- Do the managers and supervisors' managers model informal recognition practices?

- Do the managers and supervisors understand the intention and purpose of company recognition?

- Are there clear expectations set out for managers and supervisors regarding recognizing employees?

Formal Recognition

- Is there a nomination process?

- Who is eligible to nominate whom?

- Do some rewards have restrictions for eligibility (part-time vs. full-time staff)? How is this justified and communicated? What programs are available for those not eligible for some rewards?

- Are committee members eligible for formal recognition?

- How often will a formal reward be presented?

- Who makes the ultimate decision regarding the "winner"?

STEP 6: Identify Reward Choices

A critical role of the recognition committee is to provide appropriate suggestions for supervisors and managers to use when implementing either formal or informal recognition practices. It is important that each manager be free to choose recognition that is congruent with his or her values and management style, but there is also a distinct need to keep reward and recognition fairly consistent with the company as a whole. For instance, the manager in Accounting can't be rewarding high performers with trips to Hawaii if all the employees in Distribution get are T-shirts and movie passes. It is the job of the recognition committee to work with senior managers, department managers and employees to figure out what levels of reward and recognition are available and for what. As always, leave room for individual creativity but set some boundaries for managers and supervisors to follow. The second half of this book is full of great recognition and reward ideas and the following is a list or reward channels commonly used within companies:

Ceremonies:

- Luncheon or dinner

- Retirement party

- Holiday party

Gifts:

- Event tickets

- Gift certificates

- Trophies/plaques

- Monetary and paid leave awards

Publicity:

- Newsletters

- Other publications

- Departmental annual report

- Display a plaque or trophy publicly

- Letter or certificate given personally to an employee by a supervisor or manager

- Recognition at staff meeting

- Day of appreciation

STEP 7: Monitor and Enhance Program

Your recognition program needs to be monitored and evaluated on a regular basis to assess its effectiveness and to obtain feedback and suggestions from employees for enhancements to the program. The recognition program committee is the facilitator of this process but it needs to be done in conjunction with senior managers and departmental staff. Ideally there is a feedback system incorporated into the daily operations of the recognition program, but at the very least an evaluation needs to take place on a yearly basis. This last step brings us to the final stage of setting up your recognition plan: recognizing that you need to have continuous evaluation.

Acknowledge That Your Recognition Plan Requires Continuous Evaluation

Even though you have followed the process to a "T," your recognition program will not remain effective forever. The premise of this book is that motivation changes for people and over time so you must keep your program fresh and relevant at all times. This requires a commitment to continuous review and evaluation. You need to do this analysis both formally and informally. Surveys can be given out periodically but the best way to gauge the level of stagnancy is to keep your ear to the ground and remain in tune with your employees. Some common signs that your recognition program is in need of a revamping include the following:

Enthusiasm Is Lost

- Do your employees still talk about the program?

- Do they seem energized and motivated to earn recognition or reward?

- Have old habits started to creep back into the workplace?

If you answer "yes" to any of these questions, then you need to engage your employees and discuss what is going on, figure out what you need to do create excitement again, and then do it.

Participation Is Dwindling

- Are fewer nominations coming in for rewards?

- Is informal recognition waning?

- Are managers losing their motivation to participate?

An effective recognition program is supposed to breed excitement and take on a life of its own. When this positive recognition cycle ceases, you know your program needs a boost. Look at ways to encourage recognition throughout the company and make sure the recognition effort is not just top down but between coworkers and upward to managers as well.

The Program Is the Butt of Jokes and the Source of

Complaints

- Do employees run around the hallways mocking your recognition efforts?

- Is using a company coffee mug a source of hysterics?

- Do employees create mock certificates for the "Best Butt Kisser" or take coworkers out to lunch to celebrate a missed deadline?

- Is your suggestion box full of allegations of inequality and favoritism?

When employees start making fun of your recognition efforts, then you know it is no longer a source of value. And when they start complaining about the mechanics of your program, you are in big trouble. Recognition that is perceived as unfair is a prime source of employee dissatisfaction and will have an extremely negative effect on your workplace motivation efforts. Return to your mission and purpose and look at the actual operation of the program. If you need to go back to stage one, do it—do whatever it takes to keep the program valuable.

Rewards and Recognition = Expectation

- Do your employees expect the recognition perks without putting in any special effort?

This is the most insidious and dangerous of all recognition program pitfalls. It is also the hardest to detect. There is a fine line between recognizing employees for a job well done and recognizing employees for doing their job. When you start a recognition program, it is common to over-recognize— you want to catch employees doing something right. If, however, you don't replace your over-recognition with recognition that is tied to exceptional behavior (as defined by your recognition criteria), then you run the risk of employees expecting recognition for everything they do. Keep a close eye on this phenomenon and monitor yourself and others to make sure recognition remains appropriate.

Process for Program Reassessment

The beginning stage for any program change is data collection. Solicit feedback from your employees and managers through surveys, group discussion or one-on-one interviews. Find out which aspects of the program are well received, which elements are ineffective or unpopular, if there are any sources of contention with the process, who uses the program, if someone is not using the program find out why not, if the actual rewards are losing value and significance, if the mechanics of the program are problematic, etc. Gather as much information about the current usage and perception of the program as possible. You will use this data to make the changes necessary.

Once you know what the sources of ineffectiveness or dissatisfaction are, you need to make a plan to change them. Many times an infusion of new life into the program is enough to reenergize employees and managers. Brainstorm new ideas that will encourage the recognition culture in general and

try out innovative rewards and incentives. You may need to get a little wacky just to liven things up— fun is always appreciated and it certainly brings a renewed sense of energy to even the most mundane of situations.

Regardless of what specific changes or interventions you make, keep in mind that no recognition program will last forever. They all necessarily get dull after a period of time so expect to change every so often. By planning for change you won't get disheartened with the recognition effort. Make sure you keep senior management involved in the program and encourage them to participate openly in the programs efforts. There is no greater incentive than a senior role model, so make sure you have top management participation and support.

The first part of the book has given you the background and tools necessary to develop an effective process for creating a high-motivation workplace. The reasons why motivation is such an important workplace issue should be readily apparent, and I hope you are excited and enthused about bringing about the changes necessary to infuse more recognition and intrinsic motivation into your workplace. The next part of this book will examine specific ways to extrinsically motivate your employees. I alluded to many extrinsic motivation processes in the Recognition section and, when used in combination with intrinsic motivation techniques including informal recognition, formal recognition is a powerful motivator.

I hope the last half of this book will give you many

ideas and is a source of inspiration for you as you develop your own unique approach to motivation and recognition within your organization.

motivation

"Never tell people how to do things. Tell them what to do and they will surprise you with their ingenuity."

GEORGE S. PATTON,
AMERICAN MILITARY LEADER

chapter 4

INSPIRING TIPS FOR BUILDING A HIGH-MOTIVATION WORKPLACE

Management guru Peter Drucker once said, "Economic incentives are becoming rights rather than rewards." The significance of that statement on workplace motivation is that in order to get and keep employees motivated in today's work environment, you need to look beyond what they are paid and focus on recognizing them for their contributions to the organization.

The rest of this book is devoted to suggesting external motivators that you can use to enhance employee satisfaction and performance. Even after you have created a foundation for a motivation-rich workplace you can't be complacent. Motivation changes constantly and it is a dynamic process that needs continual tweaking and recharging. There are a wide variety of tools and techniques you can use that enhance the natural motivation inherent in each and every employee and I hope to provide you with a source of many alternatives from which you can choose and adapt to your employees' specific needs and preferences.

To give you an idea of how significant external rewards are to today's employees, here are the results of an Employee Motivation survey conducted by GoalManager in 2000.

EMPLOYEE MOTIVATION SURVEY

What could your company do to help make your work more meaningful?

Action	Percentage of Employees Agree
More perks and incentive programs.	18%
Pay me more.	18%
Improve recognition and rewards.	14%
Improve communications.	14%
Empowerment/Creative freedom with job.	14%

Action	Percentage of Employees Agree
I wouldn't stay once I decided to leave.	10%
More interesting work/more meaningful work.	8%
Give me a promotion and a better career path.	6%
Remove a bad manager.	5%
Provide us with better products.	5%
More structure and more definitive goals.	5%
Reduce the red tape.	4%
Professional training.	4%
Modicum of job security.	3%
Life/work balance.	3%
Respect for work.	3%
Expand clients.	3%
Better people.	3%

Action	Percentage of Employees Agree
Hold everyone accountable for their work.	1%
Pay me on time.	1%
Treat me like full-time staff.	1%
Cross-pollinate departments.	1%
Employee-suitable jobs.	1%
Family needs.	1%

The "actions" highlighted in light gray are ones that are addressed with formal, extrinsic motivation and the "actions" highlighted in darker gray are intrinsic factors discussed in the first half of this book. By combining the power of these two sources of motivation, you will tap directly into the source of positive motivation that will spur your employees' productivity and performance to levels you never imagined.

Having made my point about the power of extrinsic motivation, the following sections provide numerous specific ways for you to begin motivating your employees. Use my suggestions as a starting point and let your own creativity and knowledge of your employees come through to design reward and recognition practices that are as unique as your company and its people.

Gifts

The most common and first thought of way to reward employees is through the giving of a gift. People love gifts and they love to be surprised, what they don't love is to be surprised with a gift that is inappropriate or useless. Before you become the office Santa, look over the following gift ideas and then decide what will be most appreciated by specific employees. I've included gifts in many price ranges and most can be adapted to suit your budget requirements.

General Gift Ideas

1. **Gift certificates** – This is an old standard but it definitely ensures the recipient gets what he or she wants.

2. **Chocolates** – You can give a simple candy bar or you can create an elaborate basket of chocolates from a gourmet chocolatier.

3. **Lottery tickets** – Have scratch-and-win tickets on hand to give out as spontaneous recognition.

Consider creating a lottery fund and having all employees participate. For special recognition, purchase tickets to the larger home lotteries that are sponsored by charitable organizations. Not only do you recognize your employees but you also contribute to worthwhile causes.

4. **Dinner for two** – Who doesn't appreciate a dinner for two certificate? Make sure you choose the type of restaurant that would most suit the person receiving the reward. Some people enjoy pretentious silver service with waiters who use special crumb scrapers between courses and others prefer the more relaxed atmosphere of popular national chain restaurants.

5. **Massage certificate** – You can get a variety of massage packages from a simple foot massage to an all-over body massage or massages with herbal and aromatherapy elements. Go as fancy or plain as you think is appropriate and as your budget can handle.

6. **Prepared food service** – For busy families this type of recognition is a God-send. Chefs make and delivery pre-prepared meals that can be taken directly from the freezer, cooked and served. Most companies offer a wide range of meal choices and they are all balanced and nutritious. These services are quickly becoming the fast food of the 21st century.

7. **Catered dinner** – Have a chef come to your employee's home and prepare a gourmet meal especially for his or her family. What a treat! If you want to make it extra special, provide a catered dinner for eight so your employee can invite some friends to join in the celebration.

8. **Cookies delivered to employee's door** – Many online companies offer gourmet cookie service. You can get a weekly or monthly order and you can even try the special cookie of the month. A fun way to receive a reward that continues over time.

9. **Balloon bouquet** – Have it delivered to the office or home. If you want to make this type of recognition silly, fill the employee's office with balloons and have colleagues watch as he or she

makes his or her way to the desk.

10. **Year's supply of pantyhose** – Obviously for the females at you workplace but a much-appreciated reward. No one likes to spend money on staple items and pantyhose are about the most boring purchase women make.

11. **Certificate for tailoring** – Good for men and women, this will give them a lift as their clothes fit better and they feel better.

12. **Shoe shine services for a year** – You can get certificates or you can arrange for the shoe shiner to come to your office once a week for a period of time to shine the shoes of all employees who have earned the recognition.

13. **Beauty salon services** – Try to find out if the employee has a particular establishment she prefers and then surprise her with a certificate for a cut, color, highlight, makeover, etc.

14. **Allow a deserving employee to choose a guest speaker for your next event** – The entire organization benefits from the speaker's words and the employee is rewarded by learning about a topic that is of particular interest to him or

her. As an added touch, have the employee introduce the speaker or include him or her in the presentation in some other way.

15. **Barber certificates** – Again, determine if your employee is a regular somewhere and then prepay the barber so the next time your employee goes to get his hair cut, he will be surprised with a freebie.

16. **Spa services** – Pamper your employees who deserve it. Spas offer so many fabulous services that there should be no difficulty finding something that is just right for the person you want to recognize.

17. **Gift on the date of employee's anniversary** – This type of recognition goes beyond just giving a reward and shows that you take a personal interest in the employee. Anniversary dates are special and there is no better way to celebrate than with some token of appreciation. If your budget does not allow for a gift, a hand-written card is just as meaningful and will be valued no matter what.

18. **Gym membership** – Depending on budgets and circumstances, you may want to pay for a full-

year membership, six months, one month, or just the initiation fee. You decide, but make sure the employee will appreciate the gesture before committing him or her to an exercise regime.

19. **Workout clothes certificate** – For the athletic types in your office this is an excellent gift. Consider getting a certificate to a high-end store where the person might not shop on a regular basis but would certainly like to have one article of clothing from that particular label.

20. **Exercise machine** – This gift is certainly a high-end item but it will be a long-term source of remembrance for the employee who receives it. Every morning or evening, when the exercise begins, the recognition principle will be reinforced. Just make sure you are not forcing exercise on an employee, and find out what kind of equipment he or she prefers before making such a large purchase.

21. **A number of shares of stock** – Not only does this type of reward have real cash value, it is also a way to directly link employee performance to company performance. If you choose to award stock, make sure you chart your stock progress for employees as well. Post the information

in a visible location so that employees can see the dollar value of their reward. This can be an effective motivator for improving stock price through improved individual performance.

22. **Stamps** – Sounds kind of boring at first but you can get stamps in an array of designs, and they are an everyday staple that most people hate having to buy for themselves. This type of reward is especially valuable at the beginning of December when many employees are sending out holiday greetings.

23. **Computer software for a home computer** – Depending on your relationship with the corporate software dealer, you may be able to get a good deal on home-use software for your employees. Great ideas for software rewards are spyware and antivirus protection, home networking software, accounting packages, design suites, tax preparation software, and upgrades for common programs when they are made available. Before purchasing in volume, make sure that enough employees will use and appreciate this type of gift.

24. **Donation in employee's name to charity of his or her choice** – This is a double feel-good

kind of reward. The employee is recognized for his or her effort and a charity benefits from the recognition as well. Try to find out beforehand which charities the employee currently supports; this personal touch will make the reward that much more meaningful.

25. **Tickets to a gala** – Many times special events come to town that are invite only. If your company is on the reserved list, purchase tickets for a special employee and have him or her and their spouse attend as your guests. This will be perceived as quite an honor and the employee gets the added bonus of relaxed, out-of-the-office time with senior people from the organization.

26. **Box seats for a baseball, football, basketball or hockey game** – If you have an employee who is a sports fan, treat him or her to a game in the company box seats. While this perk is usually reserved for customers, there is nothing wrong with sharing it with employees as well.

27. **Certificate for cleaning services** – With the type of work hours many employees are putting in, a little help around the house is an excellent and unique reward. This also gives the spouse

a break and frees up time for family on a weekend.

28. **Certificate for landscaping services** – A free lawn mowing, spring thatch or fall mulch is a surprise treat for most people. Everyone likes a well-tended lawn, but make sure the employee has a house with a yard before you offer this kind of reward. If the employee lives in a condo or apartment building, you'll end up looking very foolish and your recognition effort will be ruined.

29. **Certificate for professional home or office organization services** – This is a popular personal service that is cropping up everywhere. A professional organizer will come in and help your employee organize a closet, garage, spare room or office. If you choose the office option, your company benefits from the information and practical advice as well.

30. **Certificate for cat or dog food for a year** – Great idea, just make sure the employee has a pet. You can choose other time periods as well or even a gift certificate. If

you are trying to be equitable with the type of reward, opt for a certificate because feeding a St. Bernard for a year is significantly more expensive than feeding a Chihuahua.

31. **One month payment of mortgage or rent –** What a tremendous surprise for an employee who has done something really special. Again, it's a high-ticket item but one that is sure to make a strong and lasting impression.

32. **Certificate for a portrait** – This is an item that most people don't think to purchase on their own but one that is highly likely to be appreciated by a wide variety of people. You can choose to pay for an entire portrait package or just the sitting fee depending on the budget you are working with.

33. **Income tax preparation** – This is a perfect stress-relieving reward. No one enjoys preparing their taxes and a professional service should find deductions that the average person might miss.

34. **Personalized license plates for a year** – Get input from the employee before committing him or her to a year with "#1 MPLOYE" or "YUR GR8" on the back of their car. Some people

like attention and others abhor it; some think personalized anything is tacky and others are proud. As the name suggests, personalized plates are very personal so it's safest not to surprise anyone with this type of reward.

35. **Hot-air balloon ride** – Not for the squeamish but a thrill for many employees. This is an out-of-the-ordinary gift that most people would not think to purchase for themselves.

36. **Paid session with a financial planner** – Here is another opportunity for a double whammy reward. The employee enjoys a free service that has the potential to change his financial life.

37. **Year's subscription to magazine of employee's choice** – Everyone likes magazines, you just have to make sure to fit the right magazine to the right person. *The National Enquirer* and *The Harvard Business Review* cater to a very different demographic; make sure you know which magazine is best suited to the employee you are recognizing.

38. **One-year membership to book-of-the-month club** – If your employee is an avid reader this is an excellent reward. If he or she is more a

"books on tape" type person, this reward may fall flat.

39. **One year membership to CD-of-the-month club** – Music fans in general will appreciate this type of reward. Be sure to confirm that the CD club has an adequate selection of CD's in the music genre your employee listens to the most. If they like classical and the club sends them hard rock selections every month the reward will be more of a nuisance than a delight.

40. **Airline tickets** – Another high-end item but one that is very appreciated. Make sure the tickets have flexible fly times to accommodate your employee's schedule.

41. **Certificate for limousine service** – Your employees can use this reward to treat themselves to a night on the town or simply take the kids one day and drive around town waving their heads and arms out the sunroof. It's fun, it's unique, and it's versatile; an excellent choice for almost any employee.

42. **Monogrammed briefcase, laptop carrier or attaché case** – Monogramming is a

distinguished and classy touch to any personal object. Do not use for female employees who are engaged and likely to change their last name or those who are getting or are newly divorced. Nothing is less appealing than outdated and inaccurate monogramming.

43. **Cooking lessons** – This is an excellent idea but you don't want to insult anyone. Don't give away cooking lessons to the person on your staff who fancies him or herself a galloping gourmet unless they have expressed an interest in improving their skills. Don't limit this reward to women—it will only showcase your outdated ideas that women are the ones who do most of the cooking. A safe bet for everyone is to award BBQ lessons or a lesson in cooking exotic dishes; something at which you would assume most people are not proficient.

44. **Pet grooming for a year** – Make sure the employee has a pet. You don't want the person to feel obligated to use the certificate and come into work on Monday with their hair coiffed like a toy poodle ready for the Westminster Kennel Club Dog Show.

45. **Complete automobile detailing service** –
    Ahhh, to get back that brand-new car smell.
    With a complete automobile detail, you can
    help your employee do that. A great gift for any
    employee who owns a car. For those who ride
    the bus or subway to work because they don't
    have a car, it just shows how disinterested in
    them you are and you look foolish.

46. **Car washes for a year** – Here again, great idea;
    just make sure your employee has a car. Another
    factor to consider is what type of car wash the
    employee prefers. Some people will not take
    their "baby" through an automatic car wash,
    even the touchless kind, so a bucket full of
    quarters for the coin wash will be much more
    appreciated.

47. **Birthday card, cake, gift** – Remembering an
    employee's birthday is a very personal gesture
    that makes the person feel special. You can
    choose to go all out and have a birthday
    celebration or you can simply say "Happy
    birthday." Whatever degree of celebration you
    choose, just make sure you do something.
    Mark all of your employees' birthdays on your
    calendar and set up e-mail notifications if you're
    likely to forget. Do whatever it takes to make

sure you know when an employee is having a birthday.

48. **Pay for an employee to attend a conference of his or her choice** – This is an excellent form of reward that benefits your company as well. The employee gets training he or she is interested in and the information that is learned at the conference can be shared with other employees. A good practice that you should be implementing whenever someone goes to training is to have that person make a 15- to 20-minute presentation about what he or she learned. This extra bonus of responsibility ensures that your employees don't treat training courses as paid vacation days, and everyone benefits from one person's experiences.

49. **Case of beer/bottle of wine** – This is usually an appreciated gift but check your facts first to make sure there is no history of alcohol abuse or that the person is not a recovering alcoholic.

50. **Morning coffee for a year** – Here again, observe your employee's habits. Do they actually drink coffee? Many people opt for tea or soda instead.

51. **Case of pop or bottled water** – Good, safe

gift ideas that are sure to be used by almost everyone.

52. **Filtered water for a year at employee's home** – Drinking filtered or bottled water is becoming the norm so this is sure to be an appreciated gesture. If the employee does not want the water cooler at his or her home, have a contingency plan in place so it can be put in the office.

53. **Weekend hotel stay** – This is an excellent way to encourage an employee to take a break and relax. If the employee has kids, you may want to book a stay at a hotel that has a pool and waterslides. Try to set up the reward so the dates are flexible and so that your employee can modify arrangements to suit his or her needs the best.

54. **Gas coupons** – Great for people who drive gas cars, not so good for those with diesel or propane or the new electric cars. Make sure you know what your employees need before handing out rewards you assume are useful. If you have employees who commute to work, consider purchasing them a public transit pass instead.

55. **Oil changes for a year** – For car owners this type

of service is great.

56. **Tattoo of employee's choice** (don't ask where!) – Not appropriate in all work settings, but depending on your demographics, this may be a really cool gift. If you want to really go all out, include piercing.

57. **Video/DVD rentals** – Very safe choice for spontaneous awards. Keep a stash of free rental coupons to hand out whenever the mood strikes you.

58. **Long-distance phone cards** – Another great on-the-spot recognition gift.

59. **Dry cleaning certificates** – Like dishes and laundry, dry cleaning is a necessary evil in many people's lives. While this is probably a gift alternative that is better received in an office setting rather than manufacturing or construction, don't assume it won't be appreciated. People do wear clothes for purposes other than work and there are many items around the home that need regular dry cleaning as well.

60. **Round of golf** – Remember, just because you are

an avid golfer does not mean all your employees are as well. Golf fanatics tend to think everyone is enamored with the sport, but it is wise to make sure the person actually golfs (reasonably well) before you send him or her to an exclusive golf club.

61. **Ski pass(es)** – Great idea for winter months where skiing is accessible.

62. **Weekend car rental** – Many people love to get out and drive on the weekend, so rather than putting the miles on their own car, it is a great idea to rent a car and depreciate the value of someone else's vehicle. Another option is to rent an employee a sports car or luxury sedan; something they don't drive in their daily lives.

63. **Personal trainer** – If you have an employee who is into fitness or perhaps starting a fitness program, this is a wonderful choice. Anyone who is into diet and exercise will love the attention and advice from an expert. If the person already belongs to a gym, be sure to arrange the trainer through that facility.

64. **Concierge service** – This is a unique option for those employees who seem to have everything

already. Employees can have the concierge plan parties, get concert or theatre tickets, and make dinner reservations that they might not be able to secure on their own. A very classy touch.

65. **Have soda, fruit, snacks, etc., on hand for employees at all times** – Many companies have these items stocked for customers and guests; make them available to employees as well.

66. To mark special anniversaries of service, set up committees of coworkers to work within a certain budget and come up with a **dream gift package** – This process motivates and recognizes the employee who is being honored and the employees who are part of the committee are exhilarated by the event as well.

Having trouble deciding what gift to give to whom?

There are so many different options for gift giving available and it should be clear that not all gifts are equally appropriate for all people. The best way to figure out what your employees will most appreciate is to ask them what they like by using a recognition preference profile. I've put together a very generic profile that you can use or modify for your own organization:

RECOGNITION PREFERENCE PROFILE

From time to time I would like to recognize your efforts for an outstanding job and I really want to make the reward valuable and personal. To help me figure out what it is you might like I need to know: *What is* _____ *favorite...*
Restaurant/Food
Fast food breakfast and lunch (Big Mac, fries, etc.) _____
Sit down (Red Lobster, etc.)
Pizza/Brands, toppings
Ethnic foods
Desserts/Ice cream treats
Bagels, donuts, muffins
Snack foods

RECOGNITION PREFERENCE PROFILE

Coffee brand (Coffee Beanery, Starbucks, etc.) and drink (Cappuccino, etc.)
Soda or beverages
Miscellaneous, Favorites:
Favorite kind of music
Sports teams
Flowers
Magazines
Family activity?
Malls/Dept. stores
Video stores
Bookstores
Charity or organization
Do you have a nickname?
Personal Service:
Do you belong to a gym? Which one?
Where do you go and what services do you like (manicure, haircut, etc.)? _____   _____   _____
When you think of being pampered, what do you imagine?   _____

RECOGNITION PREFERENCE PROFILE

Tell us a little about yourself: (i.e., your family, children, etc.) _____

_____

_____

_____

_____

Do you:

Collect anything?

Play sports?

Have a hobby?

Enjoy being praised?:
☐ In private   ☐ Openly   ☐ A bit of both   ☐ Bring it on

Like to be surprised?   ☐ Yes   ☐ No
                        ☐ You won't be able to surprise me!

Which of the following types of celebrations do you prefer?

Breakfasts

Lunch

Dinners

Potluck

Personal Gift

Something else _____

RECOGNITION PREFERENCE PROFILE
What is your idea of an EXCELLENT reward? _____
Have I missed anything? _____
Thanks so much. I look forward to surprising you!

Company Merchandise

Company merchandise is still one of the most prevalent forms of employee recognition. There are a vast number of companies who specialize in supplying gift items with a company logo on them. Once the realm of customer appreciation, it is clear that many employees enjoy getting these items as well. That being said, not all employees like these items. Depending on the history of how and intention of why these items were handed out, some workplaces consider them nothing more than a big joke and mock the presentation of such items.

Still, company logos do mean something to a great many employees, especially those who work for companies that are respected and that have healthy, fun and respectful work cultures.

67. **Put your logo on any or all of the following:**

- Coffee mugs
- Mouse pads
- Pens
- Pencils
- Stress balls
- T-shirts
- Sweatshirts
- Golf shirts
- Tattoos
- Rings
- Buttons
- Pins
- Rulers
- Sticky notes
- Golf balls
- Golf tees
- Towels
- Candy
- Lighters
- Note cubes
- Coasters
- Umbrellas

- Luggage
- Frisbees
- Tote bags
- Hats

- Coolers
- Footballs
- Jackets
- Fridge magnets

Time Off

Who doesn't enjoy time off from work? You don't have to give full days off to reap the benefit of being considered a fantastic boss. Sometimes an extra 10 minutes tacked onto a break is all an employee needs to feel rejuvenated and ready to go again. Time off from work does not always mean spending a day idle. Many employees enjoy the ability to work from their home or even take work outside. Just getting out of the office setting is considered a reward under the right circumstances.

Ways to Give Time Off

68. **Host a "clean-out-your-files day"** – Employees devote their day to cleaning their offices or workstations. Employees are still "working," they are just doing something that is often neglected because of other pressures and responsibilities.

69. **Allow an employee to reorganize their office**

or workstation – You know how every once in a while you need to rearrange your living room furniture, well the same applies to your office space. Placing a desk in a different position and looking at a different wall all day may be enough to light a fire in the most burnt-out employee.

70. **Hand out a "get out of work free" pass** – Use your discretion about the time increments on the passes. Hand out 15-minute passes as impromptu awards and save one-hour, half-day, and full-day passes for extra special efforts.

71. **Grant a work from home day** – If the employee's job is conducive to working at home, let him or her have break. You may or may not get the same level of output, but your employee will make up the difference upon his or her return.

72. **Hand out flex passes** – These are passes that employees can redeem for the ability to set their own hours for a day or week or other period you allow. Flexible schedules are a commonly listed perk that employees enjoy and appreciate. If it really doesn't matter if they are at their desk at 8:00 a.m., let them sleep late for a few days and

work later into the evening. The important issue is that the work gets done, not necessarily when it gets done. For employees that have a more controlled schedule; that is, receptionists who must be available to answer the phone, arrange for coverage or cover the phone yourself on a day when he or she chooses to come in late.

73. **Give an employee a surprise day off** – No pre-warning, nothing: simply tell an employee who has done an excellent job or put in outstanding work that he or she need not come into work the next day. How exhilarating for the employee and fun for you—everyone likes to get and give good surprises.

74. **Award three-day weekends** – When a day off is given on a Monday or Friday (or other day depending on the employee's schedule), the reward just seems that much better. Three days of rest is more than 50 percent better, it's at least 100 times better.

75. **Allow an employee to leave early that day or come in late the next** – You probably won't have to set any specific time. Employees who feel appreciated won't take advantage of the situation and you build trust by not being a

clock-watcher.

76. When you assign an employee a project, make the deadline clear and then allow the employee to finish the assignment in his or her own way. **If the project is completed before the deadline, the employee has the option of taking the rest of the time off**.

77. After so many years of service, offer a **sabbatical leave** for the employee to explore an area of interest.

78. **Allow employees to bank sick days and extend their vacation time.**

79. **Set up a "Donated Vacation Time" bank –** Employees can donate unused hours for others to use when they find themselves in trying personal circumstances without enough holiday time to cover their leave.

Family Acknowledgement

Employees are not the only ones affected by work life stresses and pressures. The families of the employees often need a break as well. Demonstrating your consideration for the families of your employees goes a long way toward fostering a great work environment.

The message is clear: You value your employee as a person, a person who has commitments and responsibilities beyond work, and you understand how difficult balancing those commitments can be at times.

Family Acknowledgement Ideas

80. **Present a gift to your employee's spouse after a bout of overtime.**

81. **Send tickets for your employee's family to attend a fun event, movie, play, amusement park, attraction, etc.**

82. **Send a not**e – Thank your employee's spouse for his or her support during overtime.

83. **Pay for tutoring hours for children.**

84. **Provide a certificate toward day care for young children.**

85. **Provide a certificate for elder care** – Many employees are tasked with the responsibility of taking care of older parents. This can be quite a

burden, and this type of gesture is very personal and meaningful.

86. **Pay for a family swim or skate pass for a month.**

87. **Host a family orientation for new employees with a slide show or video program and include refreshments** – Including the whole family in orientation presents your workplace as "family oriented." It says you welcome family members and are in tune with the personal as well as professional needs of your employees.

88. **Collect drawings from employee's children** or grandchildren depicting "What my Mom/Dad/Grandma/Grandpa/Aunt/Uncle does at work all day" – Compile these into a company booklet or display them for customers to enjoy.

89. **Tell staff that if they achieve "such a goal" you will call their mothers/spouse/children and tell them how great their child/husband/wife/significant other/mother/father is** – Then actually do it. Remember how proud you were of doing well on a school assignment and having your teacher tell your parents? This type of recognition taps into those same feelings

of pride and accomplishment and the family members will get a kick out of it too!

90. **Plan a "bring your family to work" day for your organization** – Be sure to include different activities for different age groups. Use activities from your new-hire orientation, tours, and even special treats in the cafeteria to help make families feel a part of the organization.

91. **Give a bonus, gift, celebration, or some other form of recognition on the birth or adoption of a child** – This is an important event in a person's life. Encourage the whole department to share in the good news. Decorate the employee's office or workspace with pink or blue and celebrate his or her return to work. If your employee is the new parent of a child, invite him or her to come into the office and show off the baby.

92. **Give a reward to employees' children who achieve all "A's" on their report card.**

93. **Plan fun summer family events** – Instead of just having a picnic or doing the normal stuff, try to come up with a twist, and be sure to include activities appropriate for all ages.

94. **Host a children's holiday party** – Have a meet Santa afternoon full of games, activities, and even a gift exchange. For Easter, host an Easter egg hunt on the grounds or at a local park.

95. **Provide a "nursing room"** – Female employees returning to work may want to continue nursing their babies and need time and privacy to pump breast milk.

96. **Provide expectant dads with a cell phone or beeper so they can be summoned at a moment's notice.**

97. **Give paid time off for bereavement leave.**

FUN AND SILLINESS

People need to have fun at work. Work is work, but it doesn't have to be dull and pedantic. The best places to work are those where people don't take themselves too seriously, they allow themselves to be goofy, and they enjoy at least one laugh a day. Fun and humor are known to be strong healers and they help people get through the toughest times. It is no wonder that infusing some enjoyment and downright fun into a workplace will liven things up and naturally decrease tension and stress. The upside of laughter and amusement is that they encourage creativity and flexibility which are all central tenants of a productive and highly motivating work culture.

Ideas to Encourage Fun at Work

98. **Have "no negativity allowed" days** – Negative comments cost "x" amount of cents or dollars. Funds are placed in jar and used for a fun activity to be enjoyed later and that everyone can participate in.

99. **Bring a Polaroid camera to work** – Occasionally and take candid pictures. Post the pictures on a bulletin board for all to enjoy. Don't deliberately embarrass anyone who you know won't appreciate it (again, you need to know your employees), but there are always one or two people at work who will make this activity worthwhile for everyone!

100. **Form a recreation committee to plan monthly**

activities.

101. **Host a company poster party for employees to create signs and posters that demonstrate the company's values** – Display them throughout your office or building and move them frequently. Encourage as much creativity as possible. You may want to reward the prizes for the "Best Poster," "Most Ethereal," "Most Artistically Challenged," "Most Creative Use of Color," "Most Frightful."

102. **Create a company or department mascot that goes along with the spirit of the company or department** – "Kidnap" other departments' mascot and send ransom notes.

103. **At your next company meeting plan, to "roast" an employee or two.**

104. **Create a poem about a certain employee's accomplishments** – Read it to him or her and post it on a bulletin board. Frame an original copy for the employee to display.

105. **Have a "Laugh a Day" bulletin board** – Display appropriate cartoons and humorous writings.

106. **Designate one room as the company "Whine Cellar,"** – The place for anyone to go who is having a bad day or wants to gripe. When someone is crabby, suggest they spend some time there.

107. **Let employees take 10 to 15 minutes "fun breaks" to blow off steam or unwind.**

108. **Host international days** – Employees bring in ethnic dishes and learn about the origins and history of the culture.

109. **Host an Ugliest Tie contest or Most Worn Shoes contest** – Give out certificates and a small prize.

110. **Have a "Show and Tell" day at work** – Encourage employees to bring in their prized possessions and explain the significance. Get them to give a bit of history

about the item. You can vote on the most unique or have a "guess who it belongs to" contest before the actual presentations.

111. **Sponsor a Tackiest Accessory contest** – The winner of these contests receives a small gift.

112. **Host a joke day** – Everyone brings in their favorite joke or cartoon and shares it with colleagues. Collect the jokes and create a joke book that employees can refer to when they need a laugh.

113. **Post yearbook photos on a bulletin board** – Hold a poll to see who has changed the most and who has changed the least. Create captions to go with the photo; for example, Girl most likely to.... and Guy most likely to ....

114. **Post baby photos** – Hold a contest to see who can identify the most employees correctly.

115. **Have a talent show at work** – You'll be surprised by who plays the accordion and who tap dances. Circulate a program and have employees match participants to talents.

116. **Bring in a clown or magician to entertain**

everyone at lunchtime.

117. **Have rock/paper/scissors contests.**

118. **Fly paper airplanes whenever the mood strikes.**

119. **Name a hallway after an employee who has done a great job.**

120. **Have dart board contests** – Make up rules and present small prizes.

121. **Create special days once a month** – Have an activity that goes along with the theme.

122. **Host a juggling day** – Bring in a juggler to teach everyone the art of juggling. Hold a contest at the end for the "Best New Juggler," Juggler With the Most Unique Technique," and "Least Likely to Be a Professional Juggler."

123. **Designate a dress purple day** (or whatever color suits your fancy) – Vote on who did the best job.

124. **Have a bubblegum day** – See who can blow the biggest bubble.

125. **Have an ice cream treat day** – Go to the nearest store en-mass at lunchtime and all buy an ice cream treat.

126. **Have a picnic day** – Tell employees to bring a bag lunch and go eat outside on the lawn or go to a park. Supply blankets, sunscreen and insect repellent if necessary.

127. **Have a crazy hat day** – Vote on the best hat or swap hats every half hour.

128. **Host a polka dot day** – See how many ways you can incorporate polka dots into your work without it being inappropriate.

129. **At employee meetings, tape certificates under chairs at random** – Whoever sits in one of the special chairs can claim their prize.

130. **Have a "What I want to be when I grow up" day.**

131. **Have employees come up with suggestions for special day themes.**

132. **Host a bake sale** – The proceeds can go to charity or for a fun workplace activity.

133. **Give your employees silly string** – Let them spray it at people who deserve it.

134. **Regularly include jokes or cartoons with memos and e-mails that you send out.**

135. **At your next meeting, hand out crazy hats that everyone must wear.**

136. **Provide staff with kazoos and have them come up with an original tune** – Give a prize to the best score.

137. **Periodically hold contests like a TV game show where employees answer questions about your operations** – This can be an individual or team event.

138. **Use an 800# service where employees call in periodically to be given randomly selected test questions** – Correct answers make them eligible for a prize. Those who get all questions right receive a reward.

139. **Create stickers of appreciation** – Stick them on employees when they have done a good job. Be as creative and wacky as you want, have fun

with the message.

140. **Have a contest with employees** – "If my company/department were a T-shirt, this is what it would say. . . . " Then have them actually design the shirt, either on a real T-shirt or on paper.

141. **Host a company Olympics** – Employees compete in activities around the office and in production to see who can complete the "event" the fastest. Events may include photocopier races, getting coffee for the boss, locating a misplaced file, unloading a pallet of product, packaging a product, etc. Offers small rewards and prizes to the winners.

HOLIDAY ACTIVITIES

Holiday Recognition Ideas

142. **Have an Easter egg hunt for employees** – Let them find candy as well as other small recognition items or coupons they can redeem for work favors later.

143. **Bring rabbits, chicks and other baby animals into the office for a day** – Invite employees'

children to visit.

144. Dress like a pilgrim for Thanksgiving.

145. Bring a turkey dish for a potluck lunch the day before the long weekend.

146. Have a "Decorate the office day" to prepare for a holiday.

147. Hold a gift exchange day.

148. Have a costume contest for Halloween.

149. Host a pumpkin carving contest – Provide a small prize to the best pumpkin.

150. Dress in red for Valentine's Day.

151. Wear stars, stripes, red, white, or blue for Fourth of July.

152. Have green-colored popcorn or ice cream on St. Patrick's Day.

153. Celebrate non-Christian holidays with employees from different ethnicities and cultures.

154. **Ask minority employees to host awareness sessions** for their specific observances and make time for all employees to attend.

BIZARRE AND LARGELY UNKNOWN "DAYS"

There are many official "days" that most of us have never heard of but they are actual, sponsored days of observance. Use these days to develop unique and fun activities for your employees to participate in. On special days or within designated months, use rewards that coincide with the item or activity being honored. For instance, January is Gourmet Coffee month, so rewards and recognitions given during January could have a coffee theme. Publicize the months and days you want to observe and then have employees come up with fun activities. Make a special note of any observances that are directly related to the work done within your organization. Make sure to have a celebration of all employees during those times.

Here is a partial list of some of the "months," "weeks," and "days" I found. See Chapter 6 for a complete 365-day listing of unique days and events.

January

- Book Blitz Month (National)

- Business & Reference Books Month

- Careers in Cosmetology Month (National)

- Clean Up Your Computer Month

- Coffee Gourmet Month (International)

- Hobby Month (National)

- Human Resource Month

- Prune Breakfast Month

- Tea Month (National) – a.k.a. Hot Tea Month

- Letter Writing Week – first week of January

- Law Enforcement Training Week (National) – second week of January

- Pizza Week (National) – second week of January

- Book Week (National) – third week of January

- Handwriting Analysis Week (National) – Observed the week containing January 23rd, John Hancock's Birthday.

- Meat Week (National) – fourth week of January

February

- African American History Month (Black History Month)

- Bake for Family Fun Month

- Bird Feeding Month (National) (Wild Bird Feeding Month)

- Candy Month

- Chocolate Month

- Friendship Month

- Snack Food Month (National)

- Umbrella Month

- School Counselors Week – (National School Counseling Week) – first week of February

- Flirting Week – first week of February

- Freelance Writers Appreciation Week – first week of February

- Pancake Week – second week of February

- National Pancake Day – Shrove Tuesday, the day before Lent.

- Engineers Week (National) – third week of February

- Random Acts of Kindness Week – third week of February

March

- Craft Month

- Frozen Food Month

- International Hamburger & Pickle Month

- Noodle Month

- Peanut Month (National)

- Social Workers Month (National)

- Federal Employees Recognition Week – first full week of March

- Procrastination Week – second week of March

- Egg Salad Week – full week after Easter Sunday

April

- Frog Month (National)

- Garden Month (National)

- Guitar Month (International)

- Humor Month (National)

- Keep America Beautiful Month

- Occupational Therapy Month

- Welding Month (National)

- Clean Out Your Refrigerator Week – first week of April

- Astronomy Week – mid-April (depends on planetary alignment)

- Wildlife Week (National) – third week of April

- Administrative Professionals Week/Day (formerly Professional Secretaries Week/Day) – last full week in April

May

- Better Sleep Month

- Egg Month (National)

- Mental Health Awareness Month

- Teacher Appreciation Month

- Health Care Administrators Week – first week of May

- Teacher Appreciation Week/Day (National) – Tuesday of first full week of May

- Gamblers Week – second week of May

- Nurses Week (National) – always observed May 6th thru May 12th (Florence Nightingale's birthday)

- Police Week (National) – May 15 is National Peace Officers Memorial Day, and the week containing May 15 is National Police Week

- Pickle Week (International) – fourth week of May

June

- Candy Month

- Dairy Month (National)

- Flag Month (National)

- Iced Tea Month (National)

- People Skills Month (International)

- Rose Month (National)

- Turkey Lovers Month

- Fishing Week (National) – first week of June

- Bathroom Reading Week (National) – second week of June

- Hug Week (National) – second week of June

- Camping Week (National) – fourth week in June

July

- American Beer Month

- Anti-Boredom Month

- Baked Beans Month (National)

- Blueberry Month (National)

- Hot Dog Month (National)

- Ice Cream Month (National)

- Read an Almanac Month

- Hug Week (July 15th – 21st) – third week of July

- Salad Week (National) – fourth week of July

August

- American Artist Appreciation Month

- Inventors Month (National)

- Peach Month

- Romance Awareness Month

- Clown Week (National) – August 1–7 each year

- Smile Week (National) – second week of August

- Friendship Week (National) – third week of August

September

- Be Kind to Editors & Writers Month

- Chicken Month (National)

- Classical Music Month

- Coupon Month (National)

- Ethnic Foods Month

- Hispanic Heritage Month

- Jazz Month

- Mushroom Month

- Rice Month

- Self-Improvement Month

- Tiger Month

- Women of Achievement Month

- Assisted Living Week (National) – second week in September

- Rehabilitation Week (National) – third week in September

- Singles Week (National) – third week in September

- Dog Week (National) – last full week of September

- Tolkien Week – last week in September

October

- Book Month (National)

- Caramel Month

- Clock Month (National)

- Computer Learning Month

- Cookie Month

- Cosmetology Month (National)

- Country Music Month

- Dental Hygiene Month (National)

- Drum Month (International)

- Hispanic Heritage Month – mid-September to mid-October

- Magazine Month (American)

- Pasta Month

- Physical Therapy Month (National)

- Pickled Pepper Month

- Pregnancy & Infant Awareness Month

- Sarcastic Awareness Month

- Customer Service Week (National) – observed the first full week of October

- Gerontological Nurses Week – first week of October

- Get Organized Week – first week of October

- Emergency Nurses Week – second week of October

- Nephrology Technologist Week (National) – second week of October

- Pet Peeve Week – second week of October

- Teller Appreciation Week – second week of October

- Business Women's Week (National Business Women's Week) – third week of October

- Reading Week – third week of October

- Character Counts Week (National) – fourth week of October

- Magic Week – fourth week of October

- Peace, Friendship & Goodwill Week – fourth week of October

November

- Hospice Month (National)

- Native-American Heritage Month (American Indian Heritage Month)

- Medical Staff Services Week (National) – first week of November

- Allied Health Professions Week (National) – second week of November

- American Education Week – observed the full week prior to Thanksgiving.

- Family Caregivers Week (National) – observed Thanksgiving Week

- Family Week (National) – observed Thanksgiving Week

- Game & Puzzle Week – fourth week of November

December

- Drunk and Drugged Driving Prevention Month

- Safe Toys and Gifts Month

- Stress-Free Family Holiday Month

- Hand-Washing Awareness Week – second week of December

For more wacky (but official) observances, visit **www.brownielocks.com** or **www.butlerwebs.com.**

EMPLOYEE HONORS

Don't just rely on the "Employee of the Month" standby: award certificates to employees for a variety of office tasks, functions, and expertise. When an employee earns a special recognition give him or her, a special name tag as well as a certificate that pronounces their accomplishment to everyone. Be as fun and creative as you want, just make sure the award you present will not embarrass the recipient or make him uncomfortable.

Ideas for Employee Awards

155. **Service Quality awards** – For those employees who consistently complete client work in a timely fashion with very high quality and who make the effort to produce excellence.

156. **Practice Development awards** – For those

employees who have put forward the most consistent effort in working together as a team to help build the practice.

157. **Streamliner awards** – For those employees who came up with the best suggestions for improving the efficiency and effectiveness of the group.

158. **Administrative Support awards** – For those employees who provide the most helpful support to others.

159. **Golden Rule awards** – For those employees who always treat others kindly and fairly, who recognize their responsibility to be part of the team, and who know that by helping others succeed the whole group benefits.

160. **Best Suggestion to Clients awards** – For those employees who saved a client money, increased profitability, found errors which could have resulted in embarrassment or penalties, reduced paperwork, or increased a client's employee's productivity.

161. **Mentors of the Year Awards** – For those employees who caused others to perform

at their best, helped them develop to their true potential, or provided a supportive environment that allowed them to take risks and accept challenges.

162. **Sustained Superior Performance awards** – Award to recognize employees who have consistently exhibited superior performance throughout the course of the year.

163. **Superior Achievement awards** – For those employees who perform substantially beyond expectations on a specific assignment or job function or for a one-time special act, service or achievement.

164. **New Horizons awards** – For those employees who provide ideas/suggestions that enhance member service, improve employee satisfaction, improve operational processes and/or reduce costs.

165. **President's Award for Service Excellence** – For those employees who have consistently contributed above and beyond what is normally expected in the area of service to members and/ or employees during the previous calendar year.

166. **President's Award for Leadership Excellence** – For those employees who have exceptional leadership within the organization and who foster an environment of service and managerial excellence.

167. **Service Anniversary awards** – For those employees who have a certain number of years of tenure with the company (5, 10, 25, etc.).

168. **Best Coverage for Colleague on Holiday awards** – For those employees who provide seamless coverage while working shorthanded or in a position not regularly held.

169. **Best Cross-Training Effort** – For those employees who learned a new skill and apply their talents to help the company

170. **Exemplary Smile** – For those employees who just bring joy to the workplace with their smile and friendliness.

171. **Corporate Morale Booster** – For those employees who always know what to say and do when a colleague needs a pick-me-up.

172. **Best Computer Glitch Fixer** – For those

employees who everyone turns to when something goes wrong with the computer!

173. **Mr./Mrs. Fix-It** – For those employees who un-stick drawers, put nails in the wall to hang new certificates, build modular office furniture, un-jam the stapler, etc.

174. **Neatest Desk** – For those employees who go home every night with all their paperwork filed away and only a blotter on their desk.

175. **Most Organized** – For those employees who can produce a document dated four years ago within five minutes of your request.

176. **Photocopier King or Queen** – For those employees who know where the extra paper is, where the toner is, how to put in new toner, and how to reduce, enlarge, collate, copy double-sided and staple automatically.

177. **Fax Machine King or Queen** – For those employees who know how where the fax template is, how to send one fax to multiple recipients, how to retrieve stored faxes, and how to send an international fax.

178. **Messiest Workplace** – For those employees whose desks look like a bomb recently exploded. In addition to the certificate, you may want to consider getting a professional organizer to help them sort out their lives.

179. **Official "Go-To Gal" or "Go-To Guy"** – For those employees who everyone "goes to" when no one else seems to have an answer.

180. **Best "Out of Office" Message on Voice Mail** – For those employees who manage to sound professional on voice mail; that is they don't sound like a drone, they don't sound too bubbly, and they don't sound like they are on a caffeine high.

181. **Most Innovative E-Mail Salutation** – For those employees who include more than their official contact information at the end of each e-mail and who also avoid trite motivational or philosophical sayings which recipients are

supposed to appreciate and ponder.

GENERAL RECOGNITION IDEAS

These recognition ideas can be adapted in any way you see fit. The whole point of employee recognition is to recognize and reward those behaviors you desire. Once you have evaluated your company's needs and current recognition efforts, you should be able to take any or all of these ideas and create something that is uniquely effective for your specific workplace.

General Recognition Ideas

182. **Give a percentage off of purchase of company-made products or services.**

183. **Give out points for good attendance or any other desirable activity** – The points are redeemable for prizes.

184. **Allow employees to participate in all personnel function decisions, hiring, training, evaluating, firing and schedules.**

185. **Pick up your employees' mail and hand deliver it.**

186. **Give out perfect attendance awards or certificates of achievement.**

187. **Provide a gift certificate to the employee with longest perfect attendance record.**

188. **Allow those with a perfect attendance record to enter a lottery for $100 or $200 gift certificate.**

189. **Leave a message on an employee's voice mail thanking him or her for an outstanding job or contribution to the team.**

190. **Mention employees' success to your own boss.** Make sure your superiors know what a great job your employees do of supporting your own work efforts.

191. **Fill a bubblegum machine with pink and black bubblegum** – Employees earn tokens to try their luck at getting a black bubblegum which earns them a reward.

192. **Screen movies once a month in your boardroom or lunchroom** – Pop popcorn and supply soda and licorice.

193. **Reimburse employees for tuition fees for courses relevant to their work** – This encourages professional development without restricting the course of study to areas you designate.

194. **Set up a video game station** – Employees earn time to play the games.

195. **Purchase a pinball or arcade game** – Employees earn tokens for free play.

196. **Keep rolls of Lifesavers on hand** – When you notice or hear about someone who really helped out in a particular situation, tie a thank-you note to the roll.

197. **Wash an employee's car** out in the parking lot.

198. **Change roles with an employee for the day.**

199. **Have only one designated parking spot in the parking lot** – Reserve it for the employee of the month.

200. **Hire temporary staff to cover essential duties when you hold meetings, conferences or functions** – This ensures all employees are able

to attend and no one feels left out.

201. **Set up "Community Service" time –**
Employees can use work hours to donate time
to worthwhile charities or community activities.

202. **Maintain a flower fund** – Send flowers to
employees and their families when the need
arises.

203. **Let an employee attend a meeting in your
place.**

204. **Give a dedicated worker a new title that better
represents their contribution.**

205. **Host personal-interest courses at lunchtime
or directly after work** – Examples include
watercolor painting, fiction writing, cake
decorating and floral design.

206. **Encourage a workaholic to leave a few hours
early.**

207. **Set up a program and recruit employees –**
Participate in a Habitat for Humanity project
or other large charitable event; encourage team
and togetherness while benefiting a great cause.

208. Host an Employee Appreciation Day.

209. Sponsor an Employee Appreciation Week.

210. Put employees in TV commercials, training videos or newspaper advertisements about your organization.

211. Host a surprise picnic for the entire team in the parking lot.

212. Create a "Hall of Fame" wall with photos of outstanding achievements, both professional and personal.

213. Be your employees' champion at work – Stick up for them and never make them scapegoats when a project did not meet expectations.

214. Reward employees with assignments you know they enjoy but don't get an opportunity to do regularly.

215. Reassign work that an employee does not enjoy.

216. Provide employees with more autonomy to determine how their work is to be completed.

217. **Encourage employees to write their own personal mission statements** – Have them share their statements at the next team or department meeting. Make sure you prepare one for yourself as well.

218. **Hire additional staff for projects that require it.**

219. **Implement job-sharing opportunities.**

220. **Provide flexible work schedules.**

221. **Rearrange your workspace so employees have more privacy.**

222. **Upgrade an employee's computer.**

223. **Upgrade an employee's office chair (executive, ergonomic, etc.).**

224. **Allow employees to rent art of their choice from a local art gallery for their office or work area.**

225. **Hold a steak-and-lobster feast after a particularly challenging project is completed.**

226. **Rotate jobs every hour on a designated day or days** – This helps people understand what their colleagues actually do day to day.

227. **Deliver an employee's paycheck in person and thank him or her for their dedication and commitment.**

228. **Write a note on an employee's paycheck envelope recognizing a particular accomplishment that week.**

229. **Rename one of the meeting rooms after the employee who has made the most notable contribution to the team during the previous 12 months.**

230. **Establish a "Q-Fund"** – Money can be used for anything that improves the overall Quality of the employee's life.

231. **Host hikes, bike tours, walks or sports games to promote teamwork and a family atmosphere.**

232. **Do laundry for employees** – They drop it off on Tuesday, pick it up on Wednesday folded and pressed.

233. **Present a stuffed "Energizer bunny" to an employee who "keeps going and going."**

234. **Present a stuffed roadrunner to an employee who manages to complete a particular rush project in record** time.

235. **Have employees create a symbol of their team** – Put it on T-shirts, mugs and caps.

236. **At department meetings have teams perform a skit related to their goals and objectives.**

237. **Lighten up on dress codes** – Insist on professional attire when meeting clients, but for days when employees will be in the office, let them wear jeans or a T-shirt.

238. **Ask an employee to act as a mentor for a new employee.**

239. **Let an employee act as supervisor for a day** – This is a reward and it also increases awareness of and appreciation for the challenges you face on a daily basis.

240. **Have employees develop presentations on what their job entails for other employees.**

241. **Name a day in someone's honor** – You can play this up as much as you want. Ideas include a recognition meeting with staff, a meal or cake, a gift presentation, a certificate presentation, even a testimonial by an internal or external customer of the employee's exceptional value laden work.

242. **Sponsor an "Ideas Day"** – Recognize and generate new ideas. Have employees spend an entire day examining ways to improve the way they work.

243. **Stock a "Thank-You Store"** – Keep it full of quick and easy recognition items that managers, supervisors and peers can use to reward other employees.

244. **Keep pre-printed "you done good" or "a pat on the back" or "bravo" note cards on hand**

for managers, supervisors and peers – Inscribe a note whenever they see something recognition worthy.

245. **Support a policy of promoting from within** – This is a reward for and it also increases awareness of and appreciation for the challenges you face on a daily basis. This lets employees know that you value their history and dedication to the company.

246. **Keep a "Four A's" jar (Acknowledge, Appreciate, Affirm, Assure)** – Fill it with wonderful, uplifting thoughts for anyone who needs one. You may also give these jars as gifts to your employees with one positive thought for every day of the year.

247. **Have a circulating trophy** or a "Pay It Forward" award – Each recipient is honored both in receiving the award, and then again in being able to select someone else they feel is worthy of some recognition.

248. **Throw a company party in someone's honor** – recognize a special achievement or service dedication.

249.**Put a deserving employee in charge of "something"** – A project, a special event, a team, etc.

250.**Hold "Five-Minute Huddles" every day** – Team or department members regroup and outline exactly what needs to be done and by whom.

251. **Share letters and feedback from appreciative clients** – Read the notes aloud and then post them in a prominent place.

252.**Establish a "Caught in the Act" system** – Supervisors, managers, coworkers, etc., give out cards when they see great work being done. After accumulating ten of these cards, the employee can "cash" them in for a reward.

253.**Have employees come up with alternative job titles that are fun or better represent what they do in the company** – For instance, a supervisor in Accounting might choose the title "Assistant to the Emperor of the Accounting Realm" or an administrative assistant might choose "Queen of Filedom." Have employees create business cards for their alter egos and use them with clients and visitors, where appropriate.

COMMUNICATION

Employees need to know what is going on within your organization. Keeping them in the loop is one of the best and least cumbersome ways to get the message out that you value them. Talk to employees on an informal basis every day, learn who they are, and share what you know about the company and its

position. When you hold official meetings, employees should not be surprised by what they hear. If you are doing a good job keeping everyone informed then people will rally behind you in tough times and celebrate with you in good times.

Communication Ideas

254. **Have regular conferences with all employees and support staff** – Try to include the CEO and other senior management whenever possible.

255. **Set up a toll-free hot line to the owner/ president/CEO** – Employees can leave any question, suggestion, etc., and they will get a response.

256. **Hold a regular meeting to tell staff what is going on and how they are doing.**

257. **Always hang charts, graphs, etc., to depict regularly how the company is doing.**

258. **Hold weekly meetings with small groups of employees**– Discuss anything that is on their minds.

259. **Hold a weekly 20-minute meeting with one employee** – Discuss anything he or she wants.

260. **Use face-to-face communication rather than e-mail whenever you can.**

261. **Make your memo, fax and e-mail templates interesting** – Add cartoons or graphic designs to convey your personality as well as message.

262. **Hold monthly employee meetings at which the financial performance of the previous month and other goals are discussed in detail.**

263. **Distribute daily reports of revenue performance** – Keep employees informed about the company's financial position.

264. **Publish a regular employee newsletter** – Include some "fun" items as well as the must-read items.

265. **When an employee submits a report for your review, write a personalized message on the report** – The employee knows you actually read it.

266. **When you bring visitors or clients to the office, make a point to introduce your employees** – Have them explain what role they play in bringing your product or service to market.

267. **When people in your organization first turn on their computers, have a message of the day pop up** – You can use a quotation on customer service, personal growth, something humorous, or even the birthdays of employees during that week.

268. **Skip the formalities in your letters and memos** – Stop using words and phrases like

heretofore, therein, hereby, please be advised, sincerely, etc. Use words that you would hear in conversation. It improves your image and makes you more accessible.

269. **Circulate customer letters praising fellow coworkers** – Scan them and e-mail the file to everyone or print them in the company newsletter. Make sure as many people see the positive feedback and encourage everyone to congratulate the employee mentioned.

270. **Place congratulatory letters in employees' files.**

271. **Use your intranet or newsletter to introduce individual employees to the rest of the organization** – Interview the employee and find out what interests them, if they have any special hobbies or talents, and what generally makes them tick.

272. **Host monthly breakfasts for employees to gather together** – They will learn what is new and coming down the pipe.

273. **Use different exits and entrances for work every day** – This way you will meet new people on a regular basis.

274. **Make a point to visit the office or workspace of someone with whom you don't have much direct interaction.**

275. **Schedule short meetings with another manager's employees** – Use the time to learn about opportunities and challenges in other departments.

276. **Give employees access to files pertaining to their work history, their jobs and their department** – Create an environment of openness where information is accessible to all and not held by only a few "chosen" ones, while still maintaining confidentiality.

277. **Move your office or workspace out of the corner and relocate to smack-dab in the middle of everything** – You'll be surprised at the increased interaction and information you glean, which help you do your job better and at the same time communicate to your employees that you are one of them.

278. **Talk, talk, talk, and talk some more!**

ORIENTATION/NEW EMPLOYEES

At no time is personal and meaningful recognition more important than when a new employee enters your workplace. First impressions really are everything, and if you relay the message loud and clear from day one that your employees are important, those employees will feel important and engaged right from the start. Orientation is so  often neglected and managers need to realize the significance that effective orientation has on future work performance and motivation.

Orientation Ideas

279. **Have several line staff call the new hire to welcome him or her to the team the day he or she starts.**

280. **Have the General Manager spend at least an hour with every new employee.**

281. **Give every employee printed business cards.**

282. **Develop a welcoming ceremony.**

283. **Send new employee flowers on their first day.**

284. **Send new employees on a scavenger hunt –** They have to find certain places and items within the office or building.

285. **Create special new employee shirts –** Other employees who see someone wearing this shirt must introduce themselves.

286. **Create a collection of company legends and success stories on video or audiotape –** Use these tapes as a source of pride for current employees and as a wonderful addition to orientation for new hires.

287. **Create a "Soft Landings" welcome kit –** Have it already on their desk when they touch down! Include necessary office supplies, a phone list, employee list and a special treat.

SUGGESTION BOX

Suggestions from employees should not be viewed as necessary evils. Often the best ideas come from those who work with the process and procedures every day. Find ways to encourage suggestions and make sure your system has a mechanism to acknowledge all suggestions received.

Suggestion Program Ideas

288. **Always find ways to get staff's input into the operation** – Just a simple suggestion box works great. Make sure pens and paper are handy!

289. **Work hard at finding a way to implement each suggestion** – Give a clear explanation why it cannot be used if that is the case.

290. **Acknowledge all suggestions, even if not implemented** – Express appreciation for the thought that went into preparing the idea.

291. **If you do implement an employee's suggestion, make sure you publicize it** – Consider giving a reward.

292. **For suggestions that are implemented and that result in cost cuts, award a percentage of**

the money saved to the employee who made the suggestion.

293. **Sponsor "The Great Idea Award" complete with certificate, pin and award or gift** – If possible, name the improvement or idea after the employee and let customers who are affected by the improvement know who was behind the suggestion.

294. **Hold an annual draw of all suggestions received** – The winner receives a reward.

295. **Always ask for input on cost-cutting measures.**

296. **Create an "Awesome Attempt" booklet of great ideas that just weren't implementable or feasible at the time** – This way the employees' efforts are appreciated and your organization has a record of ideas it can turn to in the future.

SENIOR MANAGEMENT INVOLVEMENT

Senior management support and buy-in to recognition efforts is critical for recognition to be perceived as anything more than a perfunctory gesture from the managers and supervisors. The impact of a senior official's recognition for a job well done will almost necessarily outweigh the impact of the same message delivered by the employee's day-to-day manager. It's not fair, but it's the truth. The perception is, "If these high up people take the time to thank me, I must be doing something right!" Don't fight this natural tendency, exploit it and use senior management participation to make a significant impact on your recognition and motivation efforts.

Ways for Senior Management to Get Involved

297. **Have senior managers cook employees breakfast.**

298. **Have senior managers bring around an ice cream cart.**

299. **Have senior managers serve employees doughnuts and coffee.**

300. **Have senior managers wash the windshields of employees' cars as they arrive at work.**

301. **Have senior managers take all employees to lunch.**

302. **Have senior managers make spontaneous calls to line staff saying how much they are appreciated** – Give specific reasons why.

303. **Host a "Meet the President" forum for lunch** – Make sure most employees can attend.

304. **Reward employees with a lunch with top departmental administrators.**

305. **Extend invitations to deserving employees to participate in "higher-level" meetings.**

306. **Hold an annual banquet for those with more than a certain number of years of service.**

307. **Implement management reviews where the employees assess their manager's and supervisor's performance.**

308. **Hand out VIP passes that allow an employee access to otherwise reserved areas within your company.**

309. **Set aside a day where senior managers perform front line jobs** – This is a great opportunity to interact with employees and it keeps upper manager in touch with the day-to-day opportunities and challenges faced by line staff.

310. **Hold regular face-to-face information sessions**

with employees – Answer any and all questions that come up.

PUBLICITY

People vary in the amount of publicity they want for their accomplishments. You need to respect each employee's comfort level with public praise. For those that thrive on publicity, you can really pour it on and for those who shy away from the limelight, share their accomplishments with others in a low-key manner. Recognition will quickly lose its value if it is done without regard for an employee's feelings so always keep that in mind before you single someone out for worthy accolades.

Ideas for Public Recognition

311. **At the end of the workday, plan an employee recognition ceremony** – Hold it in your conference room, kitchen or largest office space. Give an announcement/speech about the completed project and give recognition to the people who made it possible.

312. **Stand in front an employee's desk and in a loud voice, read a "decree" from a scroll of their accomplishment** – Give all your

"winners" paper crowns to wear for the day along with a reward.

313. **Get on the company intercom and announce the people and teams who reached their goal** – Have the winners meet you in the conference room, lunchroom, etc., for a short reception to celebrate the accomplishment!

314. **Rent a local billboard** – Celebrate a person's professional accomplishments and distinguished service to your organization and its clients.

315. **Take out a full-page ad in newspaper once a year** – Thank employees and name each of them individually.

316. **Start a column in your newsletter for employee recognition** – Send the newsletter to clients and keep a few extra copies to give to the employee mentioned.

317. **Tell the employees' clients about the recognition they received** – Explain what the recognition was for and thank the client for their continued support.

318. **Create a "Tree of Appreciation" for all staff** – Post congratulations, kudos and thank-yous to employees who make a difference. Place the tree in a prominent spot.

319. **Write a "Friday Fan Mail" where you thank an employee for his or her weekly contributions and accomplishments** – Send the e-mail to everyone in the organization.

320. **Post a thank-you note on an employee's or colleague's office door.**

321. **Send an e-mail message to everyone in the company advising of someone's personal contribution to your own accomplishment.**

322. **Create a "Behind the Scenes" award for those who tend to shun the limelight.**

Well, there you have it, hundreds of ideas to help you get your creative juices flowing when it comes to unique, fun, practical and sincere ways to recognize your employees and create a high-motivation workplace.

We started off this discussion about motivation by discussing intrinsic motivation and have come full circle to end with extrinsic motivators. The whole point of this book, though, is that you can't isolate these different frames of reference. They work very interdependently with intrinsic motivation forming the foundation for extrinsic motivation to be built upon. It's not enough to simply throw rewards at employees and expect them to respond positively. Your entire culture must be built on recognition and appreciation. Some forms of recognition are extrinsic but the more lasting elements are those that permeate to the core of your business of philosophy and values.

Armed with the information, tools, techniques and this book, I hope you are no longer on a search for "motivated employees" and that you understand the necessity of first building a motivating environment. I'm reminded of the line from the movie *Field of Dreams*, "Build it and they will come." It's true, if you set your workplace up as a motivation place, the people within will become motivated in the direction you desire and the people you bring in will be attracted to your workplace because of the culture and atmosphere you create.

Remember, you don't find motivated employees; you provide motivating environments for employees.

I sincerely hope you now how have a response to the question I posed to you at the very beginning of this book:

"How motivated are you to provide a motivating workplace?"

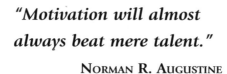

"Motivation will almost always beat mere talent."

NORMAN R. AUGUSTINE

chapter 5

FREQUENTLY ASKED QUESTIONS ABOUT REWARD AND RECOGNITION

1. **What can I do to reward my employees?**

   While monetary reward is typically the first answer that comes to mind, they are not the only (or even most) effective recognition strategy for motivating your staff. Using monetary rewards is not always possible and employees can come to expect gifts rather than "thanks," which puts you in a tough situation.

2. **If I have no money to reward my employees, what can I do?**

   There are so many non-monetary and low-cost ways to recognize and reward employees. I have included hundreds of specific ideas for recognition, but the most important factors for employee recognition are at the beginning of the book where you will learn to create a motivating foundation for your employees. Once you have done that, rewards are just the icing on the top: Nice to look at, sweet to taste, but the cake underneath is the really good part.

3. **When I try to complement or recognize my employees for little things, some of them act uncomfortable. Am I doing it right?**

In order for recognition to be effective, you need to consider the following three elements of the person and your relationship with him or her:

- Does that individual employee value the way you are recognizing him or her? All people respond differently to positive feedback, some get a real boost of pride and others shy away and are embarrassed. You need to know your employees' personalities and tailor your recognition efforts accordingly.

- Does the recognition you are providing have to do with an activity or accomplishment the employee actually values? When people think you are just saying something nice because you have to, the compliment is often interpreted as an insult. "If you can't find something good to say about my work that really matters to me, that must mean I'm not doing a good job." Make sure your recognition efforts are genuine and specific to your employee's work.

- Do you have a positive relationship with the employee you are trying to recognize? Hearing a compliment from someone you trust and respect is much better received than one from someone you find difficult to get along with. Try to establish personal, meaningful relationships with all of your employees while still respecting their personal boundaries and comfort zones.

When you address the three elements above, you should see a marked difference in the way your recognition is received.

4. **When I publicly highlight someone's work, other employees say they feel unappreciated.**

The most likely cause for this is that those other employees are feeling underappreciated and recognized. Make an effort to find something positive to say about everyone every day. You aren't obligated to keep checklists of who got recognized for what and when, but it is important to find something positive to say about everyone on a regular basis.

5. **I like to recognize my employees but my own supervisor doesn't do much recognizing of his own. What can I do get some praise myself?**

A great method to try is to recount some of your recognition efforts to your boss. Talk to him about the effectiveness of your recognition and how it has made your job much easier. Serve as a role model of recognition for your boss by recognizing his efforts. Recognition is infectious. You will see that he is much more likely to return the thanks when he realizes how good it made him feel inside to receive your compliments.

6. **What should I do when it's obvious that only some staff are doing the work of the team and I want to recognize the team effort.**

This is a tough situation and one where you need to first address why some employees are doing all the work. Perhaps you need to take a more hands-on approach and coach the slackers to improve their performance. When you know there is disparity of effort within a team, honor the team in a small way and then provide individual recognition and reward at will. You can celebrate the team's results and reward individual contributions at the same time.

7. **My staff wouldn't take me seriously if I all of sudden started praising them and thanking them**.

If you haven't been a "recognizer" in the past, then this transformation should be managed just as any other change initiative within your organization. Start by communicating why recognition is important and then discuss how you intend to start implementing the program. Start off low key and gradually build yourself up to singing their praises from the rooftop. When your employees get a firsthand glimpse at how it feels to be recognized for both large and small accomplishments, they will wonder why they thought it was foreign in the first place.

8. **What should I recognize? Excellence? Customer service? Performance improvement? Cost-saving?**

The only rule to follow is this: "What gets recognized gets done." If you want more cost savings, then start recognizing the heck out of anything your employees do to achieve it. If you want customer service excellence, then catch employees doing something nice for customers. Make sure your recognition has a direct link to the behavior you are encouraging. Don't just say "thanks," say "Thank you for helping that customer find exactly what she was looking for. I'm sure you improved her shopping experience tenfold."

9. **I am not comfortable organizing or hosting parties or public events. How can I recognize my employees?**

There are lots of other ways to recognize your employees that don't involve parties or public events. You employees will probably know and realize that you are not a high-publicity type and would not expect such recognition from you in the first place. If you think your staff would enjoy a party, solicit them to plan the event. A party is fun no matter who organizes it and the activity will give them a refreshing break from their daily routines.

10. **How do I know if I'm recognizing people the right way?**

You will know your recognition is working by three main criteria:

- Is the person receiving the recognition displaying positive and open body language?

- Has the workplace improved in terms of comfort and increased performance?

- Do you feel good after giving the recognition?

If you answer yes to the above questions, then your recognition efforts are working. If there is something lacking, go directly to the source and ask your employees what you could do better. Perhaps you are not as in tune with their individual needs, preferences and values as you need to be in order to deliver effective praise. Your recognition efforts will need to change and adapt on a regular basis, so get used to soliciting feedback on your recognition technique and put the suggestions into action.

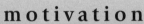

"Without credible communication, and a lot of it, employee hearts and minds are never captured.

JOHN P. KOTTER, LEADING CHANGE

chapter 6

MOTIVATION 365: A MONTHLY CALENDAR

In Chapter 4, you found hundreds of specific ideas for recognition. Now here is the inspiration to create your own. On the following pages you'll find a 12-month calendar with more unique (sometimes wacky) "events" for every day. Use these special days to celebrate and motivate your employees. Here are a few suggestions:

- January 14th is National Dress Up Your Pet Day. Invite your employees to bring in a photograph of their festooned pet and have a contest to vote for the best. Award prizes such as a free grooming or a month's supply of pet food.

- February is American Hearth Month. Bring in a cardiac specialist to assess employees' heart attack risk.

- May 13 is National Apple Pie Day. What better

reason is there treat everyone to an all-American dessert?

- June 15 is Smile Power Day. Hold a contest for who has the best smile or smiles the most all day long. Award a free dinner as a prize.

- July 24 is Amelia Earheart Day. Award your most productive employees with two free airplane tickets to the destination of their choice.

- August is Family Fun month. Hold a weekly drawing for tickets to the nearest amusement park.

- September 6 is Fight Procrastination Day. Have employees submit a project they have been procrastinating (cleaning the storerooom, tidying the breakroom) and the boss will tackle it.

- November 15 is Clean Out Your Fridge Day. Have an employee potluck lunch and provide dessert.

- December 21 is Look at the Bright Side Day. Close early and give everyone an extra hour or two of free time.

JANUARY

1	2	3	4	5	6	7
Birthdays: Betsy Ross Paul Revere	National Science Fiction Day National Cream Puff Day	Drinking Straw Day Birthday: Mel Gibson	National Spaghetti Day First Road Sign	National Whipped Cream Day	National Shortbread Day Apple Tree Day	Typewriter Patented Birthdays: Nicolas Cage Katie Couric
8 National Clean Off Your Desk Day Birthday: Elvis Presley	**9** National Apricot Day Birthday: Richard Nixon	**10** Volunteer Firemen's Day Barbed Wire Patent	**11** International Thank You Day Birthday: Alexander Hamilton	**12** National Marzipan Day First X-Ray Taken	**13** Frisbee Invented Accordion Patented	**14** Dress Up Your Pet Day Hot Pastrami Sandwich Day
15 National Strawberry Ice Cream Day Birthday: Martin Luther King Jr.	**16** National Fig Newton Day	**17** Pig Day Birthdays: Jim Carrey Muhammad Ali	**18** Jazz Day Birthday: Kevin Costner	**19** National Popcorn Day Birthday: Dolly Parton	**20** Cheese Day Basketball Day	**21** Hugging Day Birthday: Geena Davis
22 National Blonde Brownie Day	**23** Hand-writing Day National Pie Day	**24** National Peanut Butter Day	**25** Opposite Day First Winter Olympics Began	**26** National Peanut Brittle Day Birthday: Paul Newman	**27** National Chocolate Cake Day Birthday: Wolfgang A. Mozart	**28** National Blueberry Pancake Day
29 National Corn Chip Day Birthday: Oprah Winfrey	**30** National Croissant Day	**31** Child Labor Day				

National Health Month • National Oatmeal Month
National Soup Month

FEBRUARY

1	2	3	4	5	6	7
National Baked Alaska Day

Birthday: Clark Gable | Groundhog Day

Birthday: Farrah Fawcett | National Carrot Day

Wedding Ring Day | National Stuffed Mushroom Day

Birthday: Charles Lindbergh | National Weatherperson's Day | National Frozen Yogurt Day

Birthday: Babe Ruth | National Fettuccine Alfredo Day

Birthday: Laura Ingalls Wilder |
| **8** | **9** | **10** | **11** | **12** | **13** | **14** |
| Boy Scouts Day

Kite Flying Day | National Bagels & Lox Day

Birthday: Carmen Miranda | School Day

Birthday: Greg Norman | Don't Cry over Spilled Milk Day | National Plum Pudding Day | National Tortini Day

Penicillin First Used on Humans | National Heart to Heart Day |
| **15** | **16** | **17** | **18** | **19** | **20** | **21** |
| National Gum Drop Day

Birthday: Susan B. Anthony | Do a Grouch a Favor Day

Birthday: Sonny Bono | Champion Crab Races Day

Birthday: Michael Jordan | National Battery Day

Birthday: John Travolta | National Chocolate Mint Day | National Cherry Pie Day

Birthday: Cindy Crawford | National Sticky Bun Day

Birthday: Kelsey Grammer |
| **22** | **23** | **24** | **25** | **26** | **27** | **28** |
| Be Humble Day

Birthday: Drew Barrymore | International Dog Biscuit Appreciation Day | National Tortilla Chip Day

Birthday: Enrico Caruso | Hen Laid the Largest Egg

Birthday: George Harrison | National Pistachio Day

Birthday: Levi Strauss | International Polar Bear Day

Birthday: Elizabeth Taylor | Red Spots of Jupiter

Birthday: Mario Andretti |
| **29** | | | | | | |
| National Surf & Turf Day | | | | | | |

National Dental Health Month
American Heart Month • Black History Month

MARCH

1	2	3	4	5	6	7
Peanut Butter Lover's Day Birthday: Ron Howard	Old Stuff Day Birthday: Dr. Seuss	I Want You to Be Happy Day	National Poundcake Day Birthday: Knute Rockne	Stop the Clocks Day Birthday: Andy Gibb	National Frozen Food Day Birthday: Shaquille O'Neal	National Crown Roast of Pork Day
8	**9**	**10**	**11**	**12**	**13**	**14**
National Peanut Cluster Day Birthday: Micky Dolenz	National Crabmeat Day Panic Day	First Paper Money Issued Birthday: Sharon Stone	Worship of Tools Day Birthday: Lawrence Welk	Baked Scallops Day Birthday: Liza Minnelli	Uranus Discovered, 1781	National Potato Chip Day Birthdays: Billy Crystal Albert Einstein
15	**16**	**17**	**18**	**19**	**20**	**21**
Everything You Think Is Wrong Day	Everything You Do Is Right Day	St. Patrick's Day Birthday: Nat "King" Cole	Supreme Sacrifice Day	Poultry Day Birthdays: Bruce Willis Wyatt Earp	Festival of Extra-terrestrial Abductions Day	Fragrance Day National French Bread Day
22	**23**	**24**	**25**	**26** Make Up Your Own Holiday Day	**27**	**28**
National Goof-off Day Birthday: William Shatner	Organize Your Home Office Day National Chip & Dip Day	National Chocolate-Covered Raisins Day	Pecan Day Waffle Day Birthday: Howard Cosell	Spinach Festival Day	National Spanish Paella Day First Fire Engine Tested	Something on a Stick Day
29	**30**	**31**				
Coca-Cola Invented National Lemon Chiffon Cake Day	I Am in Control Day	Oranges & Lemons Day Tater Day				

American Red Cross Month • National Craft Month
National Peanut Butter Month

APRIL

1	2	3	4	5	6	7
National Sourdough Bread Day One Cent Day	National Peanut Butter & Jelly Day	Don't Go to Work Unless It's Fun Day Birthday: Eddie Murphy	National Cordon Bleu Day Birthday: Maya Angelou	National Raisin & Spice Bar Day Birthday: Bette Davis	National Caramel Popcorn Day Modern Olympics Began	No Housework Day Birthday: Russell Crowe
8	9	10	11	12	13	14
National Empanada Day International Bird Day	Chinese Almond Cookie Day First Public Library Opened	Golfers Day Birthday: Haley Joel Osment	National Cheese Fondue Day Dandelion Day	Look Up at the Sky Day Birthday: David Letterman	Blame Somebody Else Day	National Pecan Day Birthday: Sarah Michelle Gellar
15	16	17	18	19	20	21
National Glazed Ham Day Birthday: Leonardo da Vinci	Stress Awareness Day National Eggs Benedict Day	National Cheeseball Day	Juggler's Day National Animal Crackers Day	Garlic Day Birthdays: Kate Hudson Ashley Judd	Look-Alike Day Pineapple Upside-Down Cake Day	Kindergarten Day Birthday: Elizabeth II, Queen of England
22	23	24	25	26	27	28
National Jelly Bean Day Birthday: Jack Nicholson	Read to Me Day World Laboratory Animal Day	Pigs in a Blanket Day Birthday: Barbra Streisand	National Zucchini Bread Day Birthday: Al Pacino	National Pretzel Day Richter Scale Day	National Prime Rib Day Write an Old Friend Today Day	Great Poetry Reading Day Kiss Your Mate Day
29	30					
National Shrimp Scampi Day Birthday: Jerry Seinfeld	National Honesty Day Birthday: Willie Nelson					

National Garden Month
Keep America Beautiful Month

MAY

1 National Chocolate Parfait Day May Day	**2** National Truffles Day Birthday: Dwayne "The Rock" Johnson	**3** Raspberry Popover Day National Day of Prayer	**4** National Candied Orange Peel Day Birthday: Lance Bass	**5** National Hoagie Day Birthday: Tammy Wynette	**6** Beverage Day Nurses' Day	**7** National Roast Leg of Lamb Day
8 National Teacher Day Birthday: Melissa Gilbert	**9** Butter-scotch Brownie Day Birthdays: Billy Joel Candice Bergen	**10** National Shrimp Day Clean Up Your Room Day	**11** Eat What You Want Day Twilight Zone Day	**12** Limerick Day Birthdays: George Carlin Yogi Berra	**13** National Apple Pie Day Casey at the Bat Published	**14** National Dance like a Chicken Day
15 National Chocolate Chip Day Birthday: Emmitt Smith	**16** Love a Tree Day First Envelope Made	**17** National Cherry Cobbler Day	**18** Visit Your Relatives Day Birthday: Reggie Jackson	**19** National Devil's Food Cake Day Armed Forces Day	**20** Flower Day Birthdays: Cher Jimmy Stewart	**21** National Waitresses/ Waiters Day National Memo Day
22 Buy a Musical Instrument Day	**23** Penny Day Birthdays: Jewel Drew Carey	**24** National Escargot Day Birthday: Bob Dylan	**25** National Tap Dance Day Birthday: Mike Myers	**26** National Blueberry Cheesecake Day	**27** National Grape Popsicle Day Golden Gate Bridge Fiesta	**28** National Hamburger Day Whale Day
29 Escalator Patented Birthdays: John F. Kennedy Bob Hope	**30** Ice Cream Freezer Patented First Hovercraft Launched	**31** National Macaroon Day Birthday: Clint Eastwood				

National BBQ Month

JUNE

1	2	3	4	5	6	7
Doughnut Day Birthday: Marilyn Monroe	National Rocky Road Day Birthday: Jerry Mathers	Repeat Day Birthday: Tony Curtis	National Frozen Yogurt Day Cheese Day	Festival of Popular Delusions Day	National Applesauce Cake Day Birthday: Sandra Bernhard	National Chocolate Ice Cream Day

8	9	10	11	12	13	14
National Jelly-Filled Doughnut Day Vacuum Cleaner Patented	International Young Eagles Day Birthday: Michael J. Fox	National Yo-Yo Day Birthday: Judy Garland	National Hug Holiday Birthday: Vince Lombardi	Machine Day Birthday: George Bush	Kitchen Klutzes of America Day	Pop Goes the Weasel Day Flag Day

15	16	17	18	19	20	21
Smile Power Day Birthdays: Courteney Cox Helen Hunt	National Hollerin' Contest Day	Eat Your Vegetables Day	International Picnic Day Birthday: Paul McCartney	World Sauntering Day	Ice Cream Soda Day Birthday: Nicole Kidman	Cuckoo Warning Day Birthday: Maureen Stapleton

22	23	24	25	26	27	28
National Chocolate Eclair Day Birthday: Meryl Streep	National Pink Day Typewriter Invented	Museum Comes to Life Day	Log Cabin Day Birthdays: Jimmie Walker Carly Simon	National Chocolate Pudding Day	National Orange Blossom Day Birthday: Helen Keller	Paul Bunyan Day

29	30					
Camera Day Birthdays: Gary Busey Richard Lewis	Meteor Day Birthday: Mike Tyson					

National Dairy Month • National Rose Month

JULY

1 Creative Ice Cream Flavor Day Canada Day	**2** National Literacy Day Birthday: Richard Petty	**3** Stay out of the Sun Day Compliment Your Mirror Day	**4** National Country Music Day Birthday: Geraldo Rivera	**5** Work-aholics Day Birthday: P.T. Barnum	**6** National Fried Chicken Day	**7** National Strawberry Sundae Day
8 Video Games Day Birthday: Kevin Bacon	**9** National Sugar Cookie Day Birthday: Tom Hanks	**10** Wyoming Admission Day Birthday: Jessica Simpson	**11** National Cheer Up the Lonely Day	**12** National Pecan Pie Day Birthday: Bill Cosby	**13** Fool's Paradise Day Birthday: Harrison Ford	**14** National Nude Day
15 National Tapioca Pudding Day	**16** Celebrate Air-Conditioning Day	**17** National Peach Ice Cream Day	**18** National Caviar Day Birthday: John Glenn	**19** Thank Your Mother Day Birthday: Anthony Edwards	**20** Thank Your Father Day	**21** National Catfish Day Birthdays: Robin Williams Don Knotts
22 Canine Appreciation Day Birthday: Alex Trebek	**23** National Vanilla Ice Cream Day	**24** Amelia Earhart Day Birthday: Jennifer Lopez	**25** Threading the Needle Day	**26** All or Nothing Day Birthdays: Sandra Bullock Kevin Spacey	**27** Take Your Pants for a Walk Day	**28** National Milk Chocolate Day
29 Cheese Sacrifice Purchase Day	**30** Cheesecake Day Birthday: Arnold Schwarz-enegger	**31** Parents' Day Birthday: Wesley Snipes				

National Ice Cream Month

AUGUST

1	2	3	4	5	6	7
Friendship Day National Raspberry Cream Pie	National Ice Cream Soda Day Ice Cream Sandwich Day	National Watermelon Day Birthday: Martha Stewart	Twins Day Festival Birthdays: Jeff Gordon Billy Bob Thornton	National Mustard Day	Wiggle Your Toes Day Birthday: Lucille Ball	Sea Serpent Day Birthday: David Duchovny
8	**9**	**10**	**11**	**12**	**13**	**14**
Sneak Some Zucchini Onto Your Neighbor's Porch Night	National Polka Festival Birthday: Melanie Griffith	Lazy Day Birthday: Jimmy Dean	Presidential Joke Day Birthday: Hollywood Hulk Hogan	Middle Child's Day Birthday: Pete Sampras	Blame Someone Else Day	National Creamsicle Day
15	**16**	**17**	**18**	**19**	**20**	**21**
National Relaxation Day National Failures Day	Bratwurst Festival Birthdays: Madonna Kathie Lee Gifford	National Thriftshop Day Birthday: Robert De Niro	Bad Poetry Day Birthday: Robert Redford	Potato Day Birthdays: Bill Clinton Matthew Perry	National Radio Day Birthday: Connie Chung	National Spumoni Day Birthday: Kenny Rogers
22	**23**	**24**	**25**	**26**	**27**	**28**
Be an Angel Day Birthday: Valerie Harper	National Spongecake Day	Knife Day Birthday: Cal Ripken, Jr.	Kiss and Make Up Day	National Cherry Popsicle Day	Petroleum Day Birthday: Mother Teresa	World Sauntering Day
29	**30**	**31**				
More Herbs, Less Salt Day	National Toasted Marsh-mallow Day	National Trail Mix Day Birthday: Richard Gere				

Family Fun Month

SEPTEMBER

1	2	3	4	5	6	7
Emma M. Nutt Day Birthday: Lily Tomlin	National Beheading Day	Skyscraper Day Birthday: Charlie Sheen	Newspaper Carrier Day Birthday: Damon Wayans	Be Late for Something Day	Fight Procrast-ination Day Birthday: Jane Curtin	Neither Rain nor Snow Day
8	**9**	**10**	**11**	**12**	**13**	**14**
National Date Nut Bread Day Pardon Day	Teddy Bear Day Birthdays: Adam Sandler Hugh Grant	Swap Ideas Day Birthday: Arnold Palmer	No News Is Good News Day	National Chocolate Milkshake Day	Defy Superstition Day Birthday: Mel Torme	National Cream-Filled Donut Day
15	**16**	**17**	**18**	**19**	**20**	**21**
Felt Hat Day Birthday: Oliver Stone	Collect Rocks Day Birthday: David Copperfield	National Apple Dumpling Day	National Play-Doh Day Birthday: Greta Garbo	National Butter-scotch Pudding Day	National Punch Day Birthday: Sophia Loren	The Birth of the Ice Cream Cone World Gratitude Day
22	**23**	**24**	**25**	**26**	**27**	**28**
Hobbit Day Dear Diary Day	Checkers Day Dogs in Politics Day	Festival of Latest Novelties Birthday: F. Scott Fitzgerald	National Comic Book Day Birthday: Will Smith	Good Neighbor Day National Pancake Day	Crush a Can Day Birthday: Meat Loaf	Ask a Stupid Question Day
29	**30**					
Blackberries Day Birthday: Jerry Lee Lewis	National Mud Pack Day Birthday: Jenna Elfman					

Childhood Cancer Awareness Month
Cholesterol Education Month

OCTOBER

1	2	3	4	5	6	7
World Vegetarian Day Magic Circles Day	Name Your Car Day Birthday: Groucho Marx	Virus Appreciation Day Birthday: Neve Campbell	National Golf Day Birthday: Susan Sarandon	National Storytelling Festival Birthday: Kate Winslet	German-American Day Come and Take It Day	National Frappe Day Birthday: John Mellencamp
8	**9**	**10**	**11**	**12**	**13**	**14**
American Tag Day Birthdays: Matt Damon Chevy Chase	Eat More Cheese Day Birthday: John Lennon	National Angel Food Cake Day	It's My Party Day Birthday: Joan Cusack	International Moment of Frustration Scream Day	National Peanut Festival Birthday: Nancy Kerrigan	National Dessert Day Be Bald and Free Day
15	**16**	**17**	**18**	**19**	**20**	**21**
White Cane Safety Day	Dictionary Day Birthday: Suzanne Somers	Gaudy Day Birthday: Rita Hayworth	No Beard Day Birthday: Jean-Claude Van Damme	Evaluate Your Life Day	National Brandied Fruit Day Birthday: Mickey Mantle	Babbling Day Birthday: Carrie Fisher
22	**23**	**24**	**25**	**26**	**27**	**28**
National Nut Day Birthday: Jeff Goldblum	National Mole Day Birthday: Johnny Carson	National Bologna Day	Put Your Feet Up Day Birthday: Pablo Picasso	Mule Day Birthday: Hillary Rodham Clinton	Celebrate Cows Day Birthday: Emily Post	Plush Animal Lover's Day National Chocolate Day
29	**30**	**31**				
Hermit Day	National Candy Corn Day Birthday: Henry Winkler	National Magic Day Increase Your Psychic Powers Day				

Adopt a Shelter Dog Month • AIDS Awareness Month • Book Month

NOVEMBER

1	2	3	4	5	6	7
National Senior Citizens Day	National Deviled Egg Day Birthday: Marie Antoinette	Sandwich Day Housewife's Day	Waiting for the Barbarians Day	Gunpowder Day Birthday: Vivien Leigh	Saxophone Day Marooned Without a Compass Day	National Bittersweet Chocolate with Almonds Day
8	**9**	**10**	**11**	**12**	**13**	**14**
Dunce Day Birthday: Bonnie Raitt	National Sweet Tooth Day Birthday: Lou Ferrigno	Forget-Me-Not Day	Celebrate the Beauty of Nature Day	National Pizza With the Works Except Anchovies Day	National Pudding Day Birthday: Whoopi Goldberg	Operation Room Nurse Day Birthday: Prince Charles
15	**16**	**17**	**18**	**19**	**20**	**21**
National Clean Out Your Fridge Day	Button Day Birthdays: Oksana Baiul Lisa Bonet	Take a Hike Day Birthday: Danny DeVito	National Wear Brown Shoes Day	Eat a Banana Day Birthday: Meg Ryan	Absurdity Day Birthday: Bo Derek	World Hello Day False Confessions Day
22	**23**	**24**	**25**	**26**	**27**	**28**
Start Your Own Country Day	National Cashew Day Birthday: Billy the Kid	National Dine Out Day	National Parfait Day Birthday: Joe DiMaggio	Shopping Reminder Day Birthday: Tina Turner	Pins and Needles Day Birthday: Jimi Hendrix	National Chicken Soup Day Birthday: Jon Stewart
29	**30**					
Square Dance Day Birthday: Garry Shandling	Stay at Home Because You're Well Day					

Adoption Awareness Month • Alzheimer's Disease Month

DECEMBER

1	2	3	4	5	6	7
National Pie Day Eat a Red Apple Day	National Fritters Day Birthday: Britney Spears	National Roof over Your Head Day	Honk Your Horn day Birthday: Marisa Tomei	National Sacher Torte Day Birthday: Walt Disney	National Gazpacho Day Mitten Tree Day	National Cotton Candy Day Birthday: Aaron Carter
8	**9**	**10**	**11**	**12**	**13**	**14**
Take It in the Ear Day Birthday: Kim Basinger	National Pastry Day Birthday: Donny Osmond	Festival for the Souls of Dead Whales	National Noodle Ring Day	National Ding-a-Ling Day Birthday: Frank Sinatra	Ice Cream and Violins Day	National Bouil-labaisse Day
15	**16**	**17**	**18**	**19**	**20**	**21**
National Lemon Cupcake Day	National Chocolate Covered Anything Day	Underdog Day National Maple Syrup Day	National Roast Suckling Pig Day	Oatmeal Muffin Day Birthday: Alyssa Milano	Games Day	Look at the Bright Side Day National Flashlight Day
22	**23**	**24**	**25**	**26**	**27**	**28**
National French Fried Shrimp Day	Birthday: Susan Lucci	National Egg Nog Day Birthday: Ricky Martin	National Pumpkin Pie Day Birthday: Humphrey Bogart	National Whiners Day Birthday: Steve Allen	National Fruitcake Day Birthday: Marlene Dietrich	Card Playing Day National Chocolate Day
29	**30**	**31**				
Pepper Pot Day Birthday: Mary Tyler Moore	Festival of Enormous Changes at the Last Minute	National Bicarbonate of Soda Day				

Stress-Free Family Holiday Month

chapter 7

MOTIVATION RESEARCH, FACTS & STUDIES

"The difference between a successful person and others is not a lack of strength, not a lack of knowledge, but rather in a lack of will."

VINCENT T. LOMBARDI

Now that you have discovered ways to motivate your employees, I urge you to take action! Start utilizing the suggestions today. The facts and figures on the next few pages are meant to further illustrate the importance of employee motivation:

- 70% of your employees are less motivated today than they used to be.

- 80% of your employees could perform significantly better if they wanted to.

- 50% of your employees only put enough effort into their work to keep their job

  — From *Super Motivation* by Dean Spitzer, 1995.

RESEARCH STUDY

"Incentives, Motivation and Workplace Performance: Research & Best Practices"

In this study, researchers analyzed the complete body of scientific research on incentive programs and benchmarked these findings with actual business conditions through surveys and interviews with business executives whose organizations use incentives.

What they found:

- Incentive programs improve performance by an average of 22%.

- Team incentives improve performance by up to 44%.

- Incentive programs engage participants and increase interest in work.

- Incentive programs attract and retain quality employees.

- Longer-term programs outperform short-term programs.

    - Incentive programs > one year yield an average 44% performance increase.

    - Incentive programs < six months yield an average 30% performance increase.

    - Incentive programs < one week yield an average 20% performance increase.

These figures clearly show that motivational programs work. Both you and your employees will benefit. Good luck!

motivation

"Motivation is everything. You can do the work of two people, but you can't be two people. Instead, you have to inspire the next guy down the line and get him to inspire his people."

LEE IACOCCA

INDEX

"Great things are accomplished by talented people who believe they will accomplish them."

WARREN G. BENNIS